Incentive Zoning: Meeting Urban Design and Affordable Housing Objectives

Marya Morris, AICP

Table of Contents

T he rapid growth that many communities experienced throughout the 1990s has spawned interest in planning, regulatory, and development approaches and techniques that both manage growth and meet community objectives, including the improvement of community design and the provision of affordable housing. Many new plans and land development regulations now subscribe to the principles of smart growth, which include: using land resources more efficiently through compact building forms and infill development; mixing land uses; promoting a variety of housing choices; supporting walking, cycling, and transit as attractive alternatives to driving; improving the development review process and development standards so that developers are encouraged to apply the smart growth principles; and connecting infrastructure planning to development decisions to make efficient use of existing facilities and ensure that infrastructure is in place to serve new development.

Incentive zoning is a technique that has received renewed attention as communities aim to inculcate smart growth principles into planning and development processes. Incentive zoning involves a trade-off between a community and a developer. A developer gets to build a project that would not otherwise be permitted under the existing zoning regulations in exchange for providing something that is in the community's interest— something that the city would not otherwise require of the developer (Meshenberg 1976, 43). Usually, the trade-off involves a city allowing the developer to build a larger, higher-density project. This is done by increasing the allowable floor area of a project above what is permitted in the zoning ordinance or by increasing the allowable number of dwelling units in a residential development. Additionally, setback, height, and bulk standards are often allowed to be modified to accommodate the added density or, in the case of affordable housing, to reduce development costs. Waivers of specific regulatory requirements or fees—such as parking standards or impact fees—are also included as an incentive for a developer to provide various amenities.

The common types of community benefits or amenities for which state and local governments have devised incentive programs are urban design, human services (which includes affordable housing), and transit access. Some programs, particularly those that include affordable housing as a bonusable amenity, allow developers to pay cash in lieu of building or supplying the amenity for which the incentive is being provided. Some states group all types of incentives (e.g., those for urban design, affordable housing, or transit) into an umbrella statute that authorizes local governments to use innovative land-use regulations. In several states (California, New Jersey, Oregon, and Florida), the zoning and regulatory incentive statutes for affordable housing are part of a broader statewide housing program and thus are enacted separately.

Research for this report was conducted as part of APA's Growing Smart℠ project, a multi-year effort to draft the next generation of model statutes governing planning and the management of change. Model state legislation for incentive zoning and zoning bonuses will be provided in Chapter 9 of the Growing Smart℠ *Legislative Guidebook* (APA, forthcoming Spring 2001). An excerpt of a draft of the model legislation governing the use of incentives is provided in the appendix of this report.

Part 1 of this report provides a historical perspective on incentive zoning for all purposes, contains an overview of state enabling legislation, and describes the key substantive and legal issues local governments must address in crafting such regulations. Part 2 is a description of incentive zoning for urban design and smart growth implementation. Case studies from Arlington County, Virginia, Chicago, Minneapolis, New York City, and Seattle are presented to demonstrate how incentives can be used to achieve smart growth objectives. Part 3 describes the use of density bonuses for affordable housing as the chief mechanism used in several states and municipalities to implement inclusionary housing programs. Case studies from California, New Jersey, and Montgomery County, Maryland, are provided in that section.

PART 1

Historical Perspective and Statutory Overview

ZONING INCENTIVE SYSTEMS CAME INTO USE IN THE LATE 1950S AND 1960S. CITIES WERE LOOKING FOR WAYS TO ENJOIN PRIVATE DEVELOPERS IN IMPROVING THE APPEARANCE OF THE CITIES WITHOUT SPENDING PUBLIC MONEY. Planners were also looking for ways to lessen the rigidity of Euclidean zoning that, in its preoccupation with separating land uses, was resulting in sterile, sometimes dysfunctional central business districts and neighborhoods. Euclidean zoning also made it more difficult to meet social objectives, such as affordable housing and day care. What began as an experimental technique at using zoning to improve community design has mushroomed into a fairly common tool for meeting a range of planning objectives. To wit: Jerold Kayden, an attorney, Harvard University professor, and an acknowledged zoning expert, estimated that at least one-half of all cities and towns that have zoning ordinances include bonus provisions in one form or another (Kayden 1999).

In 1957, as part of a comprehensive revision of its zoning ordinance, Chicago became the first city to enact a zoning bonus system. That system encourages developers of downtown office buildings to provide public plazas and arcades in exchange for additional density. Unlike other cities that instituted bonus programs to exact public benefits from developers, the impetus for the Chicago bonus system was to stimulate development of high-rise office buildings, too many of which, in the view of the late mayor Richard J. Daley, were being built in New York rather than Chicago. The City of Chicago's enthusiasm for offering bonuses created what is now thought of as an overly permissive system that has resulted in very large buildings with minimal public benefit at the street level (Smith 1999). Beginning in 1998, Chi-

Downtown Chicago, page 17

cago planning staff undertook a comprehensive examination of the zoning bonus provisions. In July 2000, a study of the provisions was released and a draft amendment to the zoning ordinance that will substantially overhaul the process was introduced in the city council. The report and staff recommendations are presented as a case study in this report.

New York City began its zoning incentive program in 1961 and now has the most extensive system of any city. The city uses bonuses for two purposes: to secure street-level amenities, such as plazas, arcades, and shopping galleries in high-density residential and commercial districts, and to protect the character of special districts and neighborhoods, such as theater districts. The New York system, like Chicago's, is also under scrutiny in 2000.

Inclusionary housing programs and ordinances, including voluntary or mandatory density bonuses for affordable housing, first appeared in the 1960s as a policy response to exclusionary zoning practices by local governments. (Exclusionary zoning means zoning that has the effect of keeping out of a community racial minorities, low-income residents, or additional population of any kind.) The problem of housing exclusion was brought to the fore by the 1968 report to Congress (U.S. National Commission 1969) by the National Commission on Urban Problems (known as the Douglas Commission). The commission noted that large lot-size requirements (e.g., one dwelling unit per acre as a minimum in residential zones) were the most common exclusionary technique. Others include minimum floor area requirements (e.g., house size or unit size) and prohibitions on housing types (e.g., garden apartments). Despite widespread recognition of the exclusionary effects of zoning, the Douglas Commission noted indifference on the part of courts:

> Where public action—and use control—is used to exclude large numbers of persons from certain areas on the basis of economic status, size of family, or race, fundamental questions arise for a democratic society. Generally, however, the courts have refused to consider such questions in the context of land use control cases. They continue to view such cases as largely matters of police power vs. private property rights, with no consideration of broader social implications or the right of the non-parties—those that are excluded. (p. 217)

The inaction by courts ostensibly ended with the New Jersey Supreme Court decisions in *Mt. Laurel I* (*South Burlington County NAACP v. Mount Laurel*, 67 N.J. 151, A.2d 713 (1975), *cert. denied*, 423 U.S. 808 (1975)) and *Mt. Laurel II* (*South Burlington County NAACP v. Mount Laurel*, 92 N.J. 158, 456 A.2d 390 (1983)), which, with the subsequent passage of the state's Fair Housing Act, gave New Jersey municipalities the responsibility for accommodating their fair share of affordable housing and providing for a variety of housing needs, including those of low- and moderate-income households. Similar laws passed by the California legislature in 1979 and 1980 required each local government to assume its fair share of regional housing needs, to provide "regulatory concessions and incentives" to enable moderate-cost housing to be built, to zone lands at appropriate densities to meet all housing needs, and to speed-up review procedures (Schwartz and Johnston 1983, 5-6).

Nearly two decades after their inception, many states and local governments have followed the lead of California and New Jersey and have enacted inclusionary housing programs. The challenge of translating regulatory requirements into bricks and mortar still remains, as the case studies of these state programs (and that of Montgomery County, Maryland) illustrate in Part 3.

Inclusionary housing programs and ordinances, including voluntary or mandatory density bonuses for affordable housing, first appeared in the 1960s as a policy response to exclusionary zoning practices by local governments.

The authority of local governments to institute an incentive and bonus program comes from state enabling legislation (e.g., California Government Code, Section 65915; Connecticut General Statutes, Section 8-2g(a); Florida Statutes, Chapter 163.3202(3); and Maryland General Municipal Laws, Section 10603). At least 10 states have enacted legislation expressly enabling local governments to offer zoning bonuses and other incentives in exchange for certain public benefits. None of the statutes reviewed prescribe directly what types of urban design amenities local governments may require or what types of bonuses they may offer. Statutes dealing with density bonuses for affordable housing are much more prescriptive.

Some state incentive statutes, including California's, aim to achieve one specific public purpose, such as affordable housing. Many state statutes, including those in Florida, Maryland, and Rhode Island, list incentive zoning as one of the innovative techniques that local governments can include in their zoning ordinance. Other techniques include transfer of development rights, design review, and density controls. The New York statute has unique provisions that require local governments that implement incentive zoning to evaluate whether the existing public facilities that will serve the additional density can adequately accommodate that development and to also prepare an environmental impact assessment of the proposed amenities.

In addition to the inclusionary housing requirements, California has legislation that authorizes the use of density bonuses to increase development density near transit stations with the dual goal of creating mixed-use neighborhoods with a range of housing and transportation choices and reducing both vehicle miles traveled and auto emissions. The Transit Village Development Planning Act of 1994 was linked to a demonstration program of the California Department of Transportation to test the effectiveness of increasing densities of residential development in close proximity to mass transit to increase the benefit from public investment in mass transit (California Government Code 14045(a)). The demonstration program legislation requires that participating local governments have an adopted land-use plan and zoning ordinance encouraging high-density residential development near mass transit stations. Participating governments must also demonstrate how they are implementing state legislation regarding development agreements (California Government Code, Section 65864); redevelopment plans (Article 4, Section 33330 of the state Health and Safety Code); and congestion management plans (California Government Code, Section 65099).

The act enables cities and counties to prepare a transit village plan that provides for the following.

(a) A neighborhood centered around a transit station that is planned and designed so that residents, workers, shoppers, and others find it convenient and attractive to patronize transit

(b) A mix of housing types, including apartments, within not more than a quarter mile of the exterior boundary of the parcel on which the transit station is located

(c) Other land uses, including a retail district oriented to the transit station and civic uses, including day care centers and libraries

(d) Pedestrian and bicycle access to the transit station, with attractively designed and landscaped pathways

(e) A rail transit system that should encourage and facilitate intermodal service and access by modes other than single occupant vehicles

At least 10 states have enacted legislation expressly enabling local governments to offer zoning bonuses and other incentives in exchange for certain public benefits. None of the statutes reviewed prescribe directly what types of urban design amenities local governments may require or what types of bonuses they may offer. Statutes dealing with density bonuses for affordable housing are much more prescriptive.

(f) Demonstrable public benefits beyond the increase in transit usage, including all of the following:

(1) Relief of traffic congestion

(2) Improved air quality

(3) Increased transit revenue yields

(4) Increased stock of affordable housing

(5) Redevelopment of depressed and marginal inner-city neighborhoods

(6) Live-travel options for transit-needy groups

(7) Promotion of infill development and preservation of natural resources

(8) Promotion of a safe, attractive, pedestrian-friendly environment around transit stations

(9) Reduction of the need for additional travel by providing for the sale of goods and services at transit stations

(10) Promotion of job opportunities.

(11) Improved cost-effectiveness through the use of the existing infrastructure

(12) Increased sales and property tax revenue

(13) Reduction in energy consumption

(g) Sites where a density bonus of at least 25 percent may be granted pursuant to specified performance standards

Connecticut's inclusionary zoning legislation (Connecticut General Statutes, Section 8-2g(a)) allows local governments to provide developers with a special exemption from zoning density limits in districts that permit multifamily housing. The exemption is applicable where the developer agrees to build a certain number of units of affordable housing. A local housing agency is charged with administering the program and setting thresholds to determine what sales and rent prices are to be considered affordable and the income groups that would be eligible to live in such housing. Developers must enter into a development agreement with the municipality that stipulates the number of affordable housing units being provided, the sales price or rents to be charged for the units, and deeds conveying covenants that indicate that the units will remain as affordable housing for 30 years.

Florida's growth management law mandates that local governments prepare a comprehensive plan including a housing element (Florida Statutes, Chapter 163.3177(6)(f)) and enact land development regulations to implement the plan. The enabling legislation for the regulations encourages the use of innovative land development regulations, including incentive and inclusionary zoning, as well as provisions for transfer of development rights, planned unit developments, and impact fees (Florida Statutes, Chapter 163.3202(3)).

Maryland has broadly worded language in its zoning enabling legislation that permits local governments to "encourage innovation and to promote flexibility, economy, and ingenuity in development" as well as provisions authorizing increases in the permissible density or intensity of a particular use (Maryland General Municipal Laws, Section 10603). Maryland also expressly enables counties and cities to enact ordinances that "impose inclusionary zoning and award density bonuses to create affordable housing units" and "impose restrictions on the use, cost, and resale of housing . . ." (Annotated Code of Maryland, Article 66B, Section 12.01).

Minnesota's Community-Based Planning Act of 1997 contains 11 goals for local governments to address in preparing comprehensive plans, most of which are centered on smart growth principles, such as encouraging a mix of land uses, promoting compact development, increasing the amount of affordable housing, and supporting public transit (Article 4, Community-Based Planning Act, Section 1, Subdivision 2(9)). The act also created an advisory council and directed it to, among other things, develop criteria and guidelines to promote "livable" communities in the state. The council is also directed to recommend the creation of incentives to encourage local governments to develop community-based plans. According to the act, these incentives could include assistance with computerized geographic information systems, builder's remedies and density bonuses, and revised permitting processes (Article 4, Section 13, Subdivision 2(8)). The work of the council was completed in June 1998. The act lists several tools and strategies that local governments would be able to use to achieve the livable community goals, including "densities, urban growth areas, purchase or transfer of development rights programs, public investment surcharges, transit and transit-oriented development, and zoning and other official controls."

New Hampshire has a catch-all statute for innovative land-use controls that permits a local planning board or the person who administers a zoning ordinance to enact 14 different types of standards that constitute incentives, including changes to standards affecting:

- intensity and use,
- impact fees;
- planned unit development;
- cluster development;
- performance standards; and
- inclusionary zoning (New Hampshire Revised Statutes Annotated, Title 64, Section 674.21).

The statute provides no criteria or guidelines on the type or magnitude of incentive that may be provided, nor any guidance about the use of other innovative provisions that local governments are empowered to employ, with the exception of impact fees.

New York state has an umbrella incentive zoning statute that is intended to "advance the city's specific physical, cultural and social policies in accordance with the city's comprehensive plan and in coordination with other community planning mechanisms or land use techniques" (Laws of New York, General City Law, Section 81-d). The law permits municipalities to amend the zoning ordinance to include bonus provisions and to evaluate the effects of any potential incentives to ensure that the district in which any additional density will be built contains "adequate resources, environmental quality and public facilities, including adequate transportation, water supply, waste disposal and fire protection." Local governments are also required to prepare a "generic environmental impact statement" (paid for in part by the developer) to determine if the granting of incentives or bonuses will have a significant effect on the environment. In addition to the environmental review, the statute also requires local governments "to evaluate the impact of the bonus provisions upon the potential development of affordable housing gained by the provision of such incentives or bonus afforded to an applicant or lost in the provision by an applicant of any community amenity to the city."

The statute specifies procedures that must be followed by local governments in providing the incentives, including:

- descriptions of the incentives and bonuses to be provided;

- the community benefits and amenities that may be accepted from developers;

- procedures for obtaining bonuses; and

- provisions for a public hearing on the proposed project (but only if it would not otherwise be subject to a zoning hearing).

The provisions described here pertain to New York municipalities classified (because of their size and structure) as cities. The law contains separate, although virtually identical, provisions for towns and villages in New York (Laws of New York, Town Law, Section 261-b; Village Law, Section 7-703).

The Oregon statute that implements urban growth boundaries (Oregon Revised Statutes, Section 197.296(7)) enables local governments to undertake "actions or measures to ensure that adequate levels of residential development are achieved within urban growth boundaries." The actions and measures include "enacting provisions permitting additional density beyond that generally allowed in the zoning district in exchange for amenities and features provided by the developer." Other actions include an increase in zoned residential densities overall, the provision of financial incentives, and redevelopment and infill strategies. The statute also permits the "removal or easing of approval standards or procedures" in order to achieve higher densities.

Rhode Island has an all-inclusive statute (General Laws of Rhode Island, Section 45-24-33) similar to New York's that authorizes local governments to use development incentives for several purposes. The incentives provide for "increases in the permitted use or dimension [of a building or structure, for example] as a condition for, but not limited to:

(1)   increased open space;

(2)   increased housing choice;

(3)   traffic and pedestrian improvements;

(4)   public and/or private facilities; and

(5)   other amenities as desired by the city or town and consistent with its comprehensive plan" (Section 45-24-33(B)(1)).

PART 2

Incentive Zoning for Urban Design and Smart Growth

THE FIRST MATTER A LOCAL GOVERNMENT MUST ADDRESS IN CONSIDERING AN INCENTIVE PROGRAM IS WHAT HARVARD LAND-USE PROFESSOR JEROLD KAYDEN TERMS, "THE NECESSITY ISSUE." In other words, is the incentive necessary to obtain the amenity (Kayden 1992)? And, if the amenity is important enough to the public, shouldn't it be provided directly by the local government through other means rather than leaving it to chance that a developer may opt to provide it? Or should it be made an outright requirement of the developer where the amenity is intended to mitigate the impacts of high-density development? Once a local government has addressed the necessity issue and chosen to proceed, there are four key issues that a city must consider when designing its incentives (Brooks 1970). This section presents those issues with commentary from the literature.

ESTABLISHING THE PURPOSES

The reason for providing the incentives and the community's need for specific amenities should be established in the local comprehensive plan or specific plans. These policies should also be included in the statement and intent section of the zoning ordinance. Typical purposes include mitigating the impacts of large-scale development, improving the visual appearance of an area, providing open space, and encouraging the inclusion of specific land uses in the development that the community considers desirable, such as affordable housing, day care, retail stores, and theaters. This statement of purpose will also recognize which amenities should be provided by the government and which should be required of the developer.

Downtown Minneapolis, page 20

SELECTING THE DESIRED AMENITIES

The specific amenities that the public may want and that the local government chooses to require will vary depending on the type of jurisdiction and the public purposes being served. In large cities, developers have traditionally been asked to provide pedestrian plazas and arcades, and improved access to transit. Less commonly, they have been asked to provide design and streetscape improvements, such as fountains and public art, and to include certain uses in the development itself, such as ground-floor retail and neighborhood commercial uses. Cities have also given bonuses for provision of certain necessary community features, such as affordable housing and child care facilities.

From a legal standpoint, the amenities selected by local governments tend to fall into two groups: those that are justifiable on the basis of a "traditional externalities analysis" of the local government police power and those that are justifiable on the basis of a general welfare analysis of the police power (Heyman 1970, 45). Pedestrian plazas and arcades are supported by a "traditional externalities analysis" wherein there is a rational nexus between the floor area bonuses provided and the amelioration of congestion realized by the improvements required. In other words, in the case of an office building development using a bonus that increased floor area and the number of offices, wider sidewalks and arcades can accommodate the additional pedestrian traffic generated by the additional office floor area.

When the externalities analysis focuses on the local government's right to protect the public's health and safety, incentive zoning is likely to result in trade-offs that enhance the community's social, economic, and physical environment (Heyman 1970, 46). Such bonuses, which often result in the provision of day care, affordable housing, and design features (e.g., streetscape improvements and ground-floor retail space), are justified under the general welfare analysis.

In a successful bonus program, policy makers will periodically review the list of amenities that are being provided in exchange for increased density to ensure that those amenities meet the most current planning objectives of the city. Such an audit is useful both in evaluating the type, design, and location of the amenities, and in evaluating the public purpose being served.

New York, Chicago, and Seattle, in their analyses of their bonus programs, all concluded that some of the amenities, such as plazas and arcades, were poorly designed, placed, and ultimately detrimental to the overall city design. In other words, the bonuses were not meeting (or perhaps had never met) the city planning objectives even though they had been approved by the city in the first place.

In the case of Chicago, the bonuses also had become essentially an "entitlement" for developers. Thus, the planning staff's recommendation that the program be substantially overhauled (e.g., reducing allowable bonuses in some instances and requiring better design for the amenities being provided) was met with resistance at first. As of fall 2000, however, significant changes were being considered by the city council.

In Minneapolis, consensus among planning staff in late 1999 was that the bonus system, which dated back to the 1960s, had not given the city the kinds of amenities it was looking for (Wittenberg 1999). The new system, adopted in November 1999, redirects the bonuses toward achieving smart growth goals contained in the city's new comprehensive plan. (More detail on the Minneapolis bonus system is provided below.)

> In a successful bonus program, policy makers will periodically review the list of amenities that are being provided in exchange for increased density to ensure that those amenities meet the most current planning objectives of the city. Such an audit is useful both in evaluating the type, design, and location of the amenities, and in evaluating the public purpose being served.

DETERMINING THE BONUSES TO BE GRANTED

Matching an appropriate bonus to each amenity is the most complex aspect of a zoning incentive program. In general, the value of the bonus (e.g., the increase in floor area) should be proportionate to the cost to the developer of providing the amenity. If the cost of the amenity exceeds the bonus value, the developer will have no incentive to provide the amenity. From the public's point of view, a local government ideally would provide only that amount or incentive precisely necessary to encourage a developer to build to the bonusable density and to provide the amenity because the incentive itself carries a social cost (Kayden 1992, 571). Kayden notes, for instance, that construction of a proposed high-rise development that had received a floor area bonus was blocked by a public interest organization because the building would have had a "social cost" in the form of a shadow over Central Park.

Moreover, local governments have to recognize that the building density and intensities that result from developers making use of the program have to correspond with what the private real estate market is demanding in terms of building size.

Zoning bonuses themselves are based on underlying zoning densities. When such programs were new, legal experts noted the possibility of governments artificially manipulating the baseline zoning; that is, tightening regulations beyond what otherwise would be appropriate, then loosening them in return for the provision of amenities (Mandelker 1970, 18-21; Kayden 1992, 571). The opportunity for governments to "low ball" the base zoning is theoretically more likely in cases where the city has revised its entire zoning ordinance and added a bonus program to revised zoned densities. For example, the now-defunct San Francisco downtown plan, which involved rezoning major portions of the downtown area, reduced base FAR in the office district to 14 from the pre-existing range of 16 to 20 to encourage developers to apply for the bonus (Weinstein 1994). And, in fact, Seattle's 1985 incentive ordinance was accompanied by a major downzoning, where the base FAR went from 10 to 5 and the maximum height went from 400 feet to 250 feet.

Commonly, however, bonus programs are employed with existing base densities that have been in place for some time, thus diffusing the potential for argument that densities are artificially low. Plus, experience has not supported such concerns about local government abuse. In fact, evaluations of bonus systems in New York (Kayden 1992, note 36) and Chicago (Chicago 2000) have revealed that incentives have been underpriced and that developers have been granted bonuses that far exceed the value of the amenities provided. With respect to the issue of bonuses vis-á-vis market forces, in Hartford, Connecticut, which has been very slow to recover from the real estate downturn in the early 1990s, there has not been a proposal for a development large enough to meet even the maximum base density limit—let alone be large enough to qualify for bonus—since the late 1980s (Klee 1999).

The Hartford scenario raises another issue—in an environment where amenities are being provided only through incentive zoning, a soft economy will result in various public objectives not being met if other arrangements are not made (e.g., the public either mandating that amenities be provided, instituting design guidelines, or providing the amenities itself). Despite meeting some of San Francisco's objectives of improving pedestrian movement and access to transit, the city did away with its bonus system in 1980 because overall it was regarded as ineffective in promoting good urban design (Weinstein 1994). It was replaced with mandatory design standards, including a requirement for all developments to incorpo-

Matching an appropriate bonus to each amenity is the most complex aspect of a zoning incentive program. In general, the value of the bonus (e.g., the increase in floor area) should be proportionate to the cost to the developer of providing the amenity. If the cost of the amenity exceeds the bonus value, the developer will have no incentive to provide the amenity.

rate open space into most projects. The philosophy of the change was that any amenities worth encouraging with bonuses should be seen as essential to downtown development and thus should be required.

Returning to the issue of matching bonuses to amenities, several methods of calculating the value of each have been used and studied. In 1987, the City of Chicago planning staff surveyed cities that were using zoning bonuses and identified five different approaches that have been used or considered in calibrating zoning bonuses. Getzels and Jaffe (1988) summarized the work of the city of Chicago planners. The models they found are described in the following paragraphs.

Equivalent Land-Cost Model

The equivalent land-cost model compares the costs of providing the amenity to the cost a developer would incur by purchasing additional land to achieve the same overall project density allowed with the bonus. This method is used by Seattle and Bellevue, Washington, to assign bonus values to various amenities. Getzels and Jaffe (1988) reported that both cities indicated that the formula was working well at that time. The major disadvantage they noted is in determining the boundaries of the area with which to compare land values, given that values can vary widely from district to district and even block to block in a city.

Equivalent Development Rights Model

The equivalent development rights model is similar to the land-cost model, except that it considers what a developer would have to pay to acquire additional development space or rights on the open market and not merely additional land acquisition costs. This method is used by New York City for its low-income housing bonus. The development rights are calculated using the sales prices of adjacent lots or developments similar in site area and FAR to the proposed building. The bonus is determined by dividing the cost of providing the desired amenity by the equivalent development rights costs, as illustrated in the following equation:

Added square footage of building needed to compensate amenity costs = (development rights cost) divided by (cost of amenity)

Return-on-Investment Approach

The return-on-investment approach measures the potential benefits to a developer of the amenities and the bonus (for a detailed explanation, see Seyfried 1991). It assumes that developers will choose the bonus option that results in the greatest return on their investment. The aim of planners who administer the bonuses is to calibrate the bonus so that return on investment is higher than it would be otherwise, or, at a minimum, that the return on investment is the same as it would be without the bonus system. Use of this model requires knowledge of developers' economic projections made in a pro forma. Getzels and Jaffe note that this is problematic because it provides developers with an incentive to understate net operating income to obtain higher bonus ratios (Getzels and Jaffe 1988, 19).

Marginal Cost-to-Profit Approach

The marginal cost-to-profit model compares the marginal profits derived from bonus office space to the cost of the amenity that the developer chooses to provide. In essence, the cost of providing each square foot of an amenity is defrayed by the city, permitting the developer to add a specific number of square feet of bonus floor area equal in value to the square-foot cost of the amenity. As with the return-on-investment approach, data on the square-foot costs of development and projected revenues to a developer are needed to accurately price the bonused amenity. The marginal cost-to-profit approach was used by San Francisco in the 11 years it had a bonus program.

Cost-Plus Formula

Similar to the marginal cost-to-profit approach, the cost-plus formula attempts to determine the square footage of bonus space needed to compensate a developer for building a particular amenity. The methodology requires first determining the number of square feet of building needed to cover the cost of the amenity, then multiplying that figure by a conversion ratio, which is the difference between the net rentable square feet of the building and what is allowed by the base zoning. The resulting amount is multiplied by a "plus factor," which is the added incentive required to persuade the developer to construct the amenity. This approach was devised by Jerold Kayden, a professor at the Harvard Graduate School of Design, and has never been used by a city. It was intended to be used on a site-by-site basis, which circumvents the problem with the land and development rights equivalency models that require data on construction costs and revenues from comparable properties in the same district.

ADMINISTERING BONUS PROGRAMS

The central issue for a city administering a bonus program is whether to grant bonuses as of right or to use a discretionary process involving negotiation between the city and the developer. Most cities use both. In reality, even where bonuses are granted as of right, the local government typically still exercises its discretion in the site plan review or urban design review process to which most larger projects are subjected. Naturally, any on-site amenities that the developer provides would be subject to scrutiny as well. In Seattle, the size of the bonus is directly proportional to the size of the amenity provided (based on the equivalent land-cost model described above). Thus, in practice, the developer may not know the exact size of the bonus until after the city has signed off on the proposed size, orientation, and overall design of the amenities.

Early bonus programs relied heavily on negotiations. Cities had the discretion to decide both the amount of floor area or density bonuses that would be granted as well as the type and exact design of the amenities the developer would be required to provide. Negotiating bonuses allows cities to tailor the details of a bonus arrangement to the unique aspects of each particular site. The disadvantages to this approach are the same as for all discretionary land-use review processes; namely, the process typically means additional time, expense, and uncertainty for the developer, and there is the likelihood that similar properties will not be treated uniformly, which can give rise to charges of unfairness or unequal treatment (Getzels and Jaffe 1988, 11-12).

As-of-right incentive zoning spells out the precise elements of each bonus feature and its corresponding potential density gain (Lassar 1989, 12). New York City relies largely on an as-of-right system. The bonus standards are very carefully described in a city's implementing ordinance. Seattle's system is largely discretionary, but the city does provide very detailed size and dimensional standards for most amenities. In Seattle, bonuses provided for two public benefit features—major retail stores and performing arts theaters—are determined by conditional use review of the city council. For many amenities, the city provides a range of minimum and maximum area and dimensional standards. For example, in

> The central issue for a city administering a bonus program is whether to grant bonuses as of right or to use a discretionary process involving negotiation between the city and the developer. Most cities use both.

order to be eligible for a bonus, a parcel park (e.g., a vest pocket park) must be at least 3,000 square feet and no more than 7,000 square feet of contiguous space.

In an analysis of incentive zoning schemes, Mandelker noted several scenarios that elucidate the right vs. discretion problem (Mandelker 1970, 17). For example, a city may not like the developer's design of certain amenities, even if the developer complies with the formal requirements. Moreover "substantive ambiguities" inherent in design guidelines mean that explicit procedures are needed to ensure that the public gets the amenities commensurate with the bonuses being provided. Another problem noted by Mandelker has not been borne out in the last 30 years; namely, a developer may not develop the site to its fullest potential but the site still qualifies for the bonus. In reality, the base zoning that is permitted as of right is typically adequate and is at the low end of the range of what is actually desired in a given district or on a site. The additional density that is allowed via a bonus represents the maximum acceptable density at the site.

CASE STUDIES

Zoning incentives are being used extensively by local governments to meet urban design and planning objectives, such as provision of urban design amenities, human services, and transit-related improvements. As has been described, in many cases, the amenities provided by developers, while meeting the requirements of the ordinances, have fallen short of producing a high-quality urban environment where the public benefit is of equal value to the increased return on investment realized by the developer through increased density or floor area.

Some cities, including Chicago and Minneapolis, have found it necessary to evaluate their programs to determine how well the amenities being provided meet the needs of the public and to assess their impact on urban design. In Chicago, the evaluation determined that design guidelines were sorely needed to improve the appearance of the amenities being provided. The study also concluded that the gains to developers through bonuses far outpaced the public benefit of any of the amenities provided. In redrafting its bonus provisions, Minneapolis refocused the amenities to meet progressive smart growth and sustainability goals contained in the city's new comprehensive plan. In short, the bonuses offered and the amenities required by cities must be evaluated and reconsidered to ensure that they meet contemporary community planning objectives. With that in mind, we now address how incentive zoning has been used to meet state and local goals of smart growth.

Arlington County, Virginia

Two of the earliest applications of bonuses to meet smart growth objectives were in the Ballston and Rosslyn neighborhoods of Arlington County, Virginia. The extension of Metrorail service in the late 1970s prompted the county to prepare a series of station-area sector plans for the areas in the immediate vicinity of the new train stations, including Ballston. At the time, the Ballston area lacked a downtown or definable center and was regarded as ripe for redevelopment.

The Ballston Sector Plan, which was adopted by the county in May 1980, called for Ballston to be transformed into a modern housing and commercial center focused around the Metrorail station (Bernick and Cervero 1997, 220). Indeed, that has occurred in the last 20 years. A key implementation mechanism for the plan was the use of density incentives to achieve a desired built form. A seven-block area around the Metro sta-

In Chicago, the evaluation determined that design guidelines were sorely needed to improve the appearance of the amenities being provided. The study also concluded that the gains to developers through bonuses far outpaced the public benefit of any of the amenities provided.

In redrafting its bonus provisions, Minneapolis refocused the amenities to meet progressive smart growth and sustainability goals contained in the city's new comprehensive plan.

tion was designated as a coordinated mixed-use district with high permitted densities of 3.5 FAR for commercial buildings, 135 dwelling units
per acre for apartments, and a maximum of 210 dwelling units per acre for
hotels. Street-level retail uses were also required for all commercial-office
buildings within the district. The FAR for commercial buildings is allowed to be increased to 6 from 3.5 for buildings that have 50 percent or
more of their floor space as residential units.

In 1962, well before the Ballston Sector Plan process, a redevelopment
plan for the Rosslyn area of Arlington County had led to rezoning of the
area from a mishmash of low-intensity warehouses and industrial buildings to very-high-density commercial and residential development. The
county sought to capitalize on Rosslyn's proximity to downtown
Washington, D.C., Georgetown, and federal employment centers, as well
as a new Metrorail station. The resulting development, according to
Bernick and Cervero (1997), reflected the state of planning practice of the
1960s; namely, it aimed for an automobile-oriented environment with
broad boulevards, wide plazas, a skywalk system, and little street-level
pedestrian amenity or activity.

An Amended Plan for the Rosslyn Area was adopted in 1992, and new
zoning regulations followed in 1996. The amended plan "refines the vision for Rosslyn as a first-class urban center and incorporated new goals
and objectives" for development in the area (Arlington County 2000).
Under the new zoning ordinance, the base density in the downtown area
is 3.8 FAR, which means that almost every project is large enough that it
is subject to a site plan review process. Through this process, additional
density is granted to the developer, and the developer provides public
benefits and amenities.

There is a wide range of public benefits that developers may provide in
exchange for additional floor area. These include connections to transit
stations, public art, subsidies for retail parking, and streetscape improvements. The Rosslyn bonus program is unique in that additional floor area
can be granted in exchange for not only urban design benefits, but also for
off-site amenities and economic development benefits. Developers may
also receive density bonuses in exchange for cash contributions to the
Rosslyn Fund, monies from which have been used to convert a movie theater into a performing arts space and to install a wayfinding signage system in Rosslyn.

The County Board established the Rosslyn Fund in 1991 as a Trust
and Agency Account with an initial contribution of $25,000. Subsequent
funds have been contributed by developers of projects in Rosslyn as
part of their development agreement with the county. The Rosslyn
Station Area Plan Addendum of 1992 outlined future capital improvement projects related to skywalks, streetscape, and entryways to
Rosslyn. As of May 2000, some of these improvements have been made
or are in process as part of site plan projects and the county's capital improvements program.

To implement the economic development element of the Rosslyn Plan,
developers may also be granted additional density in exchange for providing high-technology upgrades within office towers. Developers of the
1801 N. Lynn project, a 24-story office tower, the first building to be approved under the new zoning ordinance, are spending $2.7 million on
"smart-building technology," including prewiring for voice, data, and
video communications, a teleconference center, and energy efficient
HVAC systems, among other features. Robert Adkinson, economic development planner with Arlington County says that, when completed, it will
be the only building of its kind in the country.

**The Rosslyn bonus program is
unique in that additional floor
area can be granted in exchange
for not only urban design
benefits, but also for off-site
amenities and economic
development benefits.**

Bernick and Cervero (1997) note that the sector plans for Rosslyn and Ballston are examples of the Washington Metro Area Transit Authority (WMATA) aggressively pursuing joint development opportunities that link transit stations to high-density, public and private development in close proximity to the stations. Although these initiatives were not characterized as transit-oriented development (TOD) plans at the time they were prepared, today they are recognized as a precursor to the TOD planning paradigm.

Chicago

As noted above, Chicago was the first city to use zoning bonuses when it adopted incentive provisions in 1957. The primary goal of the 1957 ordinance was not to obtain public amenities. Rather, it was to encourage large-scale development by making it possible to build bigger buildings (Chicago Department of Planning and Development 2000). Developers in downtown Chicago may increase the FAR from a base of 16 to 30 if they provide plazas and arcades. A 15 percent as-of-right increase in floor area is provided for buildings that adjoin a public open space, which in Chicago includes parks, the Chicago River, and even Lake Michigan.

In 1998, the city began a comprehensive analysis of its bonus provisions. A full study of the system was released in July 2000, and a draft amendment to the Chicago zoning ordinance that would significantly overhaul the system was introduced to the city council at the same time. Similar to the situation in New York and Minneapolis, which are also revamping their programs, Chicago's system has resulted in overly generous bonuses vis-á-vis the amenities received in exchange, and it has been only marginally successful in meeting the city's needs with regard to design and public improvements.

The 2000 study by the city Department of Planning and Development identified six major problem areas with the system:

1. The ordinance awards huge FAR increases for minimal amenities. Under current regulations, a ground-floor plaza on a building with a base FAR of 16 would qualify for three separate bonuses, all of which could be "stacked" onto the base building. It would receive: a bonus of 10 FAR for a 20-foot, full-height building setback; a 6.83 FAR increase for upper-story setbacks; and a 1.14 FAR increase for ground-level open space. This would bring the total allowable FAR to 33.97, and more than double the size of the building.

2. No design standards are prescribed for open space amenities. The only requirement for open space amenities under the current system is that they be "suitably paved and landscaped." Many of the open spaces that have been provided in return for added FAR are unusable and unappealing to people.

3. Some bonusable amenities are of questionable value. Some of the amenities for which bonuses are provided no longer reflect the best approach to urban design and community aesthetics. Arcades are the feature most commonly criticized (not just in Chicago, but Minneapolis and New York too). Arcades disrupt the continuity of street-level retail uses and often terminate at blank walls, creating dark unpleasant environments for pedestrians. The lack of design guidelines has also contributed to their misuse as loading areas, service ramps, and areas for mechanical storage.

4. The menu of bonusable amenities does not adequately address the city's needs. Chicago has many needs in the downtown that the bonus system could be designed to provide. Such things include more public open space, additions to the Chicago Riverwalk, urban heat island reduction, better designed parking structures, historic preservation, and transit improvements.

Marya Morris

In some cases in Chicago, areas that should have been designed as public open space in exchange for increased floor area have instead been used for trash receptacles or loading areas..

EXAMPLE OF FAR INCREASE DUE TO MULTIPLE BONUSES

Assuming a 20-story building proposed on the same 25,000-square-foot site with a 12,500-square-foot plaza and 20-foot building setbacks along lot lines, the FAR can be increased as follows:

Basic FAR	12.00
20-foot building setback along 3 street frontages	6.00
Ground-floor open area bonus	1.32
Upper-floor open area bonus	3.96
Total FAR:	23.28

Allowable Floor Area:

Without bonus:	300,000 square feet
With bonus:	582,000 square feet

By combining all the bonuses, the base FAR has nearly doubled.

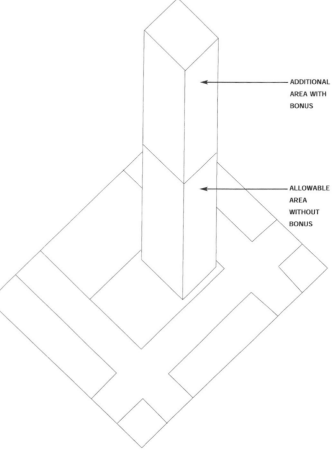

ADDITIONAL AREA WITH BONUS

ALLOWABLE AREA WITHOUT BONUS

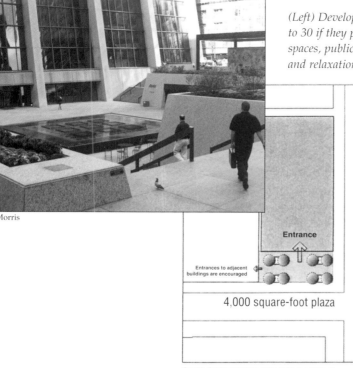

Morris

(Left) Developers in downtown Chicago may increase the FAR from a base of 16 to 30 if they provide plazas and arcades. (Below) In neighborhoods that lack open spaces, public plazas and parks offer residents and workers opportunities for rest and relaxation in open, bright landscaped spaces.

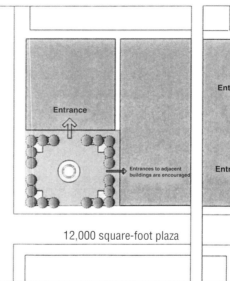

Entrance

Entrances to adjacent buildings are encouraged

Entrance

Entrances to adjacent buildings are encouraged

4,000 square-foot plaza

12,000 square-foot plaza

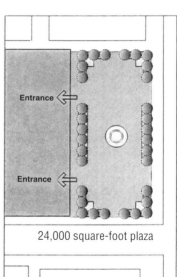

Entrance

Entrance

24,000 square-foot plaza

South-facing plazas with 30% landscaping or water features.

Marya Morris

Developers who opt to participate in Chicago's adopt-a-landmark program provide money to owners of nearby designated historic landmarks for substantial interior or exterior renovation work.

5. Density "pricing" is much lower in Chicago than in other cities that have bonus systems. The Chicago planning staff reviewed bonus systems in "peer cities" and found Chicago to have the most permissive system of any major city. (See Table 2–1 on pages 22-23.) A ground-level plaza in Chicago could earn an FAR bonus equivalent of 100 percent, whereas in New York it would earn a 20 percent bonus. The study notes that "the generosity of the present bonus system makes it difficult for Chicago officials to bargain aggressively with developers during planned development negotiations" (City of Chicago 2000).

6. The current negotiated, ad hoc bonus system is unpredictable and unfair. Most large projects in Chicago where bonuses and amenities are exchanged go through the planned development process. Although the city and developers do benefit from the flexibility the process provides, it has led to piecemeal decision making with very little predictability.

The new bonus system proposed in Chicago aims to improve the existing system by adding some new amenities to meet the city's current needs, to more closely link the value of the bonus floor area with the amenities provided, and to institute design guidelines for the plazas, arcades, and amenities. The bonuses will be capped at a maximum of 6 FAR for public plazas and pedestrian parks, which will be the highest bonus allowed. Multiple bonuses for one design feature, such as the example above where the one plaza was eligible for three bonuses, will be eliminated. "Green roofs," (i.e., rooftop gardens designed to help mitigate the urban heat island) are a new option eligible for a .30 FAR increase. And cash contributions for five types of off-site improvements, including an adopt-a-landmark provision, would also be provided. Developers who opt to participate in the adopt-a-landmark program would provide money to owners of nearby designated historic landmarks for substantial interior or exterior renovation work.

Several building design features were considered for bonuses but were ultimately omitted from the proposed amendments. Ground-floor retail, for example, which is a bonusable amenity in numerous other cities, was not added to the list because the city believes that, if it is important enough in high-density areas, it should be provided as a practice rather than an exception worthy of a bonus.

Minneapolis

Minneapolis has had provisions for zoning "premiums" (the term the city uses for bonuses) in place since 1960. Like many other cities, Minneapolis offered floor area bonuses in the downtown for street-level plazas and arcades. It also provided floor area premiums for pedestrian connections to parking garages, sidewalk canopies to protect pedestrians from inclement weather, and off-street parking and loading. These provisions met the planning objectives of the era in which they were enacted; namely, they were aimed at improving design in an automobile-oriented downtown. But as was true in other cities, the quality of the amenities being provided was not considered high, and changes needed to be made to the ordinances.

The plan for Downtown Minneapolis 2010 (an excerpt appears in the sidebar) was adopted in 1996. It addresses the use of zoning premiums in the central business district. The planning process provided the city with the opportunity to rethink the bonus system to ensure that it meets the city's up-

CONTINUING THE VISION INTO THE 21ST CENTURY
An Excerpt From the Downtown Minneapolis 2010 Plan

Implementation: Zoning

Revising the downtown zoning will be an important part of the process of implementing the land-use and development recommendations of this plan. Revising the code will enable the city to ensure the highest standards for new development while protecting the private investment that already has been made in downtown.

The City is currently comprehensively revising its zoning code. The current code needs to recognize the changes in the nature of development as well as the physical changes that have occurred withing the City over the past 30 years.

The current zoning code divides most of downtown (excluding the Loring Park and Elliot Park neighborhoods) into 13 zoning districts and subdistricts. The boundaries and standards of these districts should be revised and updated to reflect the recommendations contained in this plan. Particular attention should be paid to the following:

- Revise the organization and boundaries of the B4 districts to reflect current development patterns and objectives for future growth.

- Revise the parking requirements to balance transit policies with the goals of retaining a compact core and providing parking to met projected demand.

- Revise the bonus system to more effectively match bonuses with amenities that benefit the public and develop design standards to ensure quality results.

Bonuses for the following should be evaluated:
- Street-level retail (beyond what might be required in certain districts)
- Weather-protected bus stops that are incorporated into office and retail development
- Large urban plazas or parks; smaller plazas and parks; indoor atriums designed for public use
- Short-term parking
- Indoor public display areas for art or cultural exhibits
- Develop standards for street-level development such as street-level retail, street-level building design, and parking lot landscaping.
- Develop a residential mixed-use zoning district for downtown residential districts.
- Revise the T and TC Districts to reflect projected demand in the Minnesota Technology Corridor.
- Incorporate a Transfer of Development Rights mechanism for designated historic buildings.
- Revise the approvals process in order to achieve an understandable and efficient process.

Responsibility: City Planning Department, Downtown Council

Street-level arcades were removed from the list of bonusable amenities when Minneapolis revised its system in 1999.

Indoor open spaces, such as the Crystal Court in the IDS Center in downtown Minneapolis, are required to be open to the public during normal business hours.

dated planning objectives. To implement the plan, the city adopted a new zoning ordinance in November 1999, which includes several major changes to the bonus program. Bonus floor area may now be granted in exchange for 11 types of amenities, including public outdoor open space, interior through-block connections, pedestrian connections to the city's extensive skyway system, public art, historic preservation, and ground-floor retail. Ground-floor retail is also mandated in some parts of downtown through an overlay district. Floor area premiums range from an increase in the FAR of one—for through-block connections, skyway connections, transit facilities, widened sidewalks, and street-level retail—up to eight for projects that include outdoor open space.

Blake Graham, the city's planning supervisor, says the first order of business in drafting the

new premium standards was to remove street-level arcades from the list of amenities for which bonus floor area would be granted. Graham joked that, before the arcade bonus was eliminated, he had been tempted on occasion to grant a developer a bonus if they would agree *not* to include such an arcade. (Such a "trade-off" actually did happen in Chicago on more than one occasion.) Added to the list of bonuses is a mixed-use retail provision.

The new ordinance provisions also contain design standards regulating the location and appearance of the amenities to be provided. The city's planning director or the director's designee is charged with administrative review of all applications for premiums. In that capacity, the director does have discretion to approve alternatives to the proscribed standards; those decisions may be appealed to the planning commission. Large projects in the downtown must go through site plan review. The appendix to this report includes an excerpt of the new premium provisions in the Minneapolis ordinance.

Jason Wittenberg

The Minneapolis system provides bonus floor area for buildings that make connections to the city's famed skyway system (above). Street-level retail—with awnings or canopies for weather protection—may also garner additional floor area for office towers (right).

Jason Wittenberg

Table 2–1.HEIGHT AND DENSITY LIMITS AND ZONING INCENTIVES IN MAJOR U.S. OFFICE MARKETS, 1998

CITY	METRO OFFICE MARKET (millions of square feet)	ZONING BONUS SYSTEM	BONUSABLE AMENITIES	BULK/HEIGHT LIMITS[1]	HIGHEST BUILT FAR
Boston	143.8	Limited	Bonus (typically 2 FAR plus additional height) for participation in "large project review"	4 to 10 FAR for downtown districts. 155-foot height limit as of right with large project review bonus; 400-foot limit achievable through PD process.	Not known
Atlanta	91	Yes	• Bonus of 55 square feet of office space per 1 square foot of residential space. • 100 square feet of office space per 1 to 2 square feet of public open space.	3 to 5 FAR in most downtown districts; 10 to 25 FAR if within overlay districts centered on rapid transit stations (generally 1,500-foot radius). Wider sidewalks mandated in overlay districts.	Not known
San Francisco	84	Limited	For existing construction only, limited bonus for provision of affordable housing. Seldom used. More extensive bonus program repeated in 1984.	5 to 9 base FAR in downtown districts; by purchasing unused development potential from other sites within a given district, maximum FAR of 18 is obtainable	Approximately 24 (pre-1984)
Philadelphia	83	Yes	FAR bonus of 8 if building provides all of following: frontage on at least two streets, landscaped public space (can be enclosed), public art, retail space. On certain streets, additional bonuses up to maximum of 4 for observation decks, through-block connections, transit or park improvements, housing fund contributions, etc. TDR from historic sites permitted. Retail space, day care facilities, etc., do not count toward FAR.	Base FAR of 12 in highest density district; maximum of 24 with bonuses, although see below. No overall height limit, but height limits apply on certain streets. Additional 20 percent FAR allowed for TDR south of Chestnut Street; judging from ordinance, this is above and beyond 24 FAR limit.	Not known
Denver	70	Yes	Bonuses for downtown housing, historic preservation, childcare facilities, "residential support facilites,"schools, "pedestrian activity uses" (e.g., storefronts), "sunlight preservation," outdoor art, etc. 1.5 to 4 square feet of additional space allowed per 1 square foot of amenity; qualifying outdoor art earns 0.25 FAR bonus. additional FAR obtainable through TDR.	17 FAR limit, unless 50 percent of building is residential, in which case 20 FAR limit. No height limit in downtown core; 400-foot height limit in one peripheral downtown area (transitions to residential area), 200-foot in another (preserves mountain views).	Approximately 15
Seattle	53	Yes	Various "public benefit features," e.g., low-income housing, transferred development rights, either are not counted against FAR or earn FAR bonus.	450-foot height limit in downtown districts. Base FAR 5; can be increased to 14 through bonuses in highest density districts.	28 (Columbia Seafirst Center)

Table 2–1. HEIGHT AND DENSITY LIMITS AND ZONING INCENTIVES IN MAJOR U.S. OFFICE MARKETS, 1998

CITY	METRO OFFICE MARKET (millions of square feet)	ZONING BONUS SYSTEM	BONUSABLE AMENITIES	BULK/HEIGHT LIMITS[1]	HIGHEST BUILT FAR
New York	462.7	Yes	Bonuses are offered for arcades, open plazas, covered pedestrian spaces, subway improvements, and other public amenities. Bonuses vary by zoning classification; special bonuses apply in defined districts (e.g., midtown). Additional FAR obtainable through transfer of development rights (TDR).	No overall height limits apply in some lower-density special districts. Base FAR of 15 in highest density districts; maximum FAR of 18 with bonuses. Development rights may be transferred from adjacent structures, typically landmarks, by special permit; no limit to obtainable FAR. In TDR districts, adjacency not required, but 21.6 FAR limit applies.	Approximately 26 (several pre-1961 buildings); 21.6 max since 1961
Washington, D.C.	243.7	Yes	Bonuses provided for "preferred uses" (e.g., department stores, theatres) at a rate of 1.3 square feet of floor space per 1 foot of preferred use space. TDR program permits unused FAR from renovated historic buildings to be transferred to 1 of 5 "receiving zones" outside downtown.	130-foot height limit (street width plus 20 feet) except for certain blocks on north side of Pennsylvania Avenue, where 160-foot limit applies; however, other limits apply to these blocks Base FAR of 10 in highest districts; may be increased to 10.5 with bonuses.	Approximately 11
Dallas	175 (Includes Fort Worth)	Yes	For building setback beyond 10-foot minimum requirement. Six square feet of additional floor space permitted for each square foot of additional ground floor open space, up to max FAR of 24.	Base FAR of 20 in downtown districts; maximum FAR 24. No statutory height limit.	Approximately 25 (Nations Bank received variance)
Houston	167	No; there is no zoning	NA	No statutory limits. Houston has no zoning ordinance	Approximately 27 (1.7 million-square-foot building on 62,500 square-foot site)
Chicago	163	Yes	In business districts: • arcades • full-height setbacks • groundfloor open space • upper story setbacks In residential districts: • reduction in units • adjacent to public open space	No statutory height or bulk limits. Base FAR of 16 in highest density districts. FARs of 33+ achievable with bonuses.	32.7 (Three First National Plaza)
Los Angeles[2]	158	Limited	"Transfer of floor area ratio" (same as TDR) permitted in CBD redevelopment area, where base FAR is 3 or 6; transfer entails payment of exaction fee to city. Projects within 1,000 feet of transit station eligible for 20 percent reduction in parking requirement.	13 FAR in highest density districts. No overall height limit; height limits apply in certain areas (e.g., historic perservation districts).	17 (Library Tower; see note 2)

1. "Bulk/Height Limits" refers to statutory limits in the municipal zoning code or equivalent. In some cities, practical limits may apply to some properties due to FAA limits, private deed restrictions, sewer restrictions, and the like.

2. In Los Angeles, FAR of 17 was granted to 73-story Library Tower by special ordinance in which several building lots near LA Central Library were consolidated for purposes of density calculation; FAR of entire site including Library Tower is 11.8.

Source: City of Chicago

Once plazas are constructed, it takes ongoing monitoring to ensure that they remain open to the public. This one, at 90 Washington Street in New York City, provides little if any benefit to the neighborhood.

New York

The use of zoning bonuses has had its most profound impact on the built environment of New York City. That program, in place since 1961, has resulted in more than 500 public plazas, arcades, and open spaces at about 325 commercial and residential towers (Kayden 2000).

The city of New York uses density bonuses in high-density districts in two ways. First, they are used to provide street-level amenities in high-density residential and commercial districts, including plazas, arcades, and shopping galleries. Second, bonuses are used to protect the neighborhood character of certain districts. In residential and commercial districts, developers receive either floor area bonuses or are allowed

The lively plaza at 1755 Broadway in New York City serves both the building's tenants and passersby very well.

to reduce lot sizes in exchange for a plaza or arcade (New York City Zoning Resolution, Section 23-16-18).

In lower-density residential districts, floor area bonuses are available in exchange for deep front and wide side yards. In most cases, the bonuses are available as of right. Bonuses for large residential developments and buildings that contain community facilities (e.g., a library or a museum) are subject to a special permitting procedures—similar to a planned unit development review process—through which the developer and the city negotiate the amenities and bonuses to be provided. All residential projects that incorporate bonuses are subject to mandatory streetscape urban design guidelines (Weinstein 1994). Arcades, for example, must run the length of a block and cannot be terminated by a blank wall, although they can be interrupted by a pedestrian plaza.

Incentive zoning regulations are also applied in special districts in New York City to help achieve certain planning objectives. These districts are areas deemed to have special character or specific development issues, such as theater districts, tourist areas, and mixed-use shopping and residential districts. Additional regulations—including the zoning bonuses—are applied as overlay regulations in these districts. The purpose of the Special Midtown District, for example, which was enacted in 1980, is (1) to encourage intensive development in some subdistricts, such as Times Square, (2) to protect and preserve various Broadway theaters (many of which were being demolished and replaced with office towers), and (3) to protect the overall character of the theater district. The same basic types of amenities are provided in special districts in exchange for increased floor area, but the exact requirements and design guidelines are specific to each special district and even further refined within subdistricts. Moreover, some of the special districts also apply transfer of development rights to shift development and density from one part of the district to another.

In 1999, the city began its Unified Bulk Program, which includes (1) a study of problems of building height and bulk that have resulted from the city's existing zoning regulations, and (2) a draft comprehensive revision to the city's zoning resolution that is intended to clarify rules regarding the height and bulk of large buildings throughout the city. Part of the program involves an examination of the height and bulk problems caused by the too generous allowances given through zoning bonuses. For example, the study notes that "floor areas bonuses for residential plazas and certain other public spaces have too often produced larger buildings without providing meaningful public benefits" (New York City 1999). Moreover, plazas for residential high-rises have been privatized for enjoyment by building residents—they do not serve the general public as open space. Under the draft revision, bonuses would no longer be provided for residential plazas, with the exception of residential projects in high-density commercial districts areas, where bonuses are allowed by special permit. Bonuses for commercial and community facility plazas, which are of greater value because of the public nature of the buildings, would be retained.

Seattle: The Denny Triangle Neighborhood
Seattle has provided zoning bonuses, which the city refers to as "public benefit features," in its downtown since the early 1980s. The 28 public benefit features that developers may provide in exchange for additional development density include the common ones, such as shopping atriums, plazas, affordable housing, and transit station access. There is also a long list of unique features that includes rooftop gardens, hill climb as-

Incentive zoning regulations are also applied in special districts in New York City to help achieve certain planning objectives. These districts are areas deemed to have special character or specific development issues, such as theater districts, tourist areas, and mixed-use shopping and residential districts. Additional regulations—including the zoning bonuses—are applied as overlay regulations in these districts.

Zoning bonuses and transferable development rights are being used to transform the Denny Triangle neighborhood in downtown Seattle from a mix of underused, low-density commercial and industrial sites into a high-density, mixed-use center.

sists, sculptured building tops, short-term parking, and green streets. A green street is a street right-of-way that is part of the city's street circulation pattern that has been improved through sidewalk widening, landscaping, traffic calming, and pedestrian-oriented features. Improvements to green streets may qualify for a zoning bonus.

The state of Washington's Growth Management Act of 1990 required that Seattle and other cities update their comprehensive plan to meet statewide goals for growth over a 20-year period. Seattle's comprehensive plan, *Toward a Sustainable Seattle,* was adopted by the city council in 1994 (Seattle 2000). The plan called for future growth in the Puget Sound region to be concentrated in the city's 37 neighborhoods. The plan established a neighborhood planning process that involves nongovernmental neighborhood planning associations to prepare their own plans.

The Denny Triangle neighborhood is an area adjacent to downtown Seattle that is relatively underdeveloped.

The comprehensive plan designated the area as an "urban center village," which, to paraphrase the technical definition, meant that the area was considered to have the greatest potential of the city's five downtown neighborhoods to accommodate much more residential density than what existed there at the time. Specifically, the city plan suggested a target of 3,778 additional housing units to be built in that area, which contained only about 1,000 people when the plan was prepared.

Seattle's downtown housing program allows commercial developers to increase their permitted FAR and add commercial square footage by earning housing bonus credits through either a cash option (e.g., payments to a housing trust fund in lieu of building housing) or a production option (e.g., the developer builds both the housing and the commercial space).

The Denny Triangle Neighborhood Plan calls for the city to rezone the area to permit higher densities and taller buildings in certain areas, and to use zoning bonuses and transfers of development rights to generate moderate-income housing in the area. Specifically, the plan calls for the city to provided a "super bonus" above what was already provided for (1) the first 300 housing units servings residents in the 50 to 80 percent median-income range, and (2) the first 200 units serving residents in the 80 percent to 120 percent median-income range. The neighborhood plan noted that the area contains only low-income and low-to-moderate-income housing, thus the bonuses should be used to promote a mix of housing prices, particularly moderate-income housing. Developers are given additional commercial development capacity in exchange for the housing and other public amenities provided.

CRITIQUES OF INCENTIVE PROGRAMS AND LEGAL ISSUES

There have been very few legal challenges to incentive zoning programs, most likely because such arrangements are generally beneficial to developers, allowing them to build at higher densities and achieve profits that are greater than what may otherwise result with the underlying zoning. Plus, even when bonuses are provided as of right, incentive zoning is an elective rather than mandatory land-use control (Getzels and Jaffe 1988, 14).

In some cases, developers have expressed legitimate concern that the underlying zoned density is set artificially low to arm twist them into providing amenities to increase the size of the project to an economically feasible level. But as long as the base zoning does not extinguish reasonable development rights under the ordinance, developers would have difficulty proving that their investment-backed expectations had been thwarted. Also, through planning, communities can establish a solid rationale for linking the amenity to the mitigation of impacts created by additional density (Getzels and Jaffe 1988, 15).

The use of incentives also raises the issue of uniformity of treatment. Allowing density for a given project to be increased above what is permitted by the base zoning in exchange for certain amenities understandably leads to questions about the legitimacy of the underlying zoned densities. A developer of a similarly situated property that was completed prior to enactment of bonuses may ask why his developable density was limited to begin with. Moreover, residents of buildings adjacent to bonused buildings may question if the public benefit conferred by the developer (e.g., a public plaza) is adequate compensation to them or the general public for something like the loss of sunlight that occurs because of the added height of the new building.

Another concern is what Jerold Kayden refers to as "privately owned public space." When a developer enters into an agreement with a city to provide an amenity, such as a street-level plaza, in exchange for increased floor area, the developer also consents to allow the plaza to be open to the public. For indoor bonusable spaces, such as a through-block shopping arcade, the building owner must agree to allow the public in the space during normal hours of operation. What Kayden found in an extensive study of such spaces is that, gradually, building owners privatize the public space by: using gates to restrict public access; opening cafes and restaurants in the space, which gives the perception that it is private space; or otherwise find ways to discourage people from simply hanging around. The issue is one of enforcement, but building and zoning enforcement of-

The use of incentives also raises the issue of uniformity of treatment. Allowing density for a given project to be increased above what is permitted by the base zoning in exchange for certain amenities understandably leads to questions about the legitimacy of the underlying zoned densities.

ficers simply have higher priorities than to police the use of these spaces. One possible solution: establish a public space conservancy and use volunteers to inspect the spaces and report violations to the city.

A final issue, which has been addressed above to a certain degree, is that local government objectives change, and bonus programs need to be regularly adapted to those changes. As the twentieth century ends, many communities are refocusing their plans and land development regulations to meet smart growth objectives, including encouraging compact development, developing town centers in suburbs that lack them, mixing land uses to shorten trips and reduce car trips overall, expanding housing choices, and promoting pedestrian and bicycle facilities. Incentive zoning is a tool that should be applied directly to meet these objectives.

PART 3

Zoning Incentives for Affordable Housing

NCLUSIONARY ZONING IS A MEANS OF REMEDYING THE ECONOMIC SEG- REGATION IN HOUSING THAT HAS RESULTED FROM DECADES OF LOCAL GOVERNMENTS' WIDESPREAD USE OF LARGE-LOT ZONING, LARGE MINI- MUM HOUSE SIZES, AND THE NEAR EXCLUSION OF MULTIFAMILY OR OTHER AFFORDABLE HOUSING (Roberts 1986, Sec. 3A.01). Given the vacuum of local initiative to solve affordable housing shortages, several states enable or require local governments to adopt inclusionary zoning provisions for affordable housing (see, for example, California Government Code, Sections 65913-65918; Connecticut General Statutes, Section 8-2g; Annotated Code of Maryland, Article 66B, Section 12.01; New Hampshire Revised Statutes, Section 674:21; General Laws of New York, Town Law, Section 261- b and Village Law, Section 7-703; Code of Virginia Annotated, Section 15.1-491.9). Common tools included in inclusionary housing programs and ordinances are mandatory set-aside provisions, density bonuses, and waiving or relaxing certain regu- latory requirements. Such techniques are essentially regulatory "fixes" for a societal problem that the free market does not readily address—the pro- vision of housing for low- and moderate- income households.

Local land-use regulations are a commonly named culprit in making housing unaffordable. Among the techniques that are considered to have a exclusionary effect: minimum lot area requirements; minimum floor area requirements; limitations on multi- family dwellings and manufactured housing; minimum yard, setback, and bulk requirements; overzoning (e.g., devoting a dispro- portionate amount of land area to low-density, single-family use); and

Montgomery County, page 42

29

Research for this report indicates overwhelmingly that density bonuses and regulatory waivers, in and of themselves, do not lead to the creation of affordable housing units. Such techniques are used most effectively in concert with direct subsidies and where there is adequate land zoned to accommodate housing of all types and for all income groups.

growth management caps (Callies et al. 1999). In a study of inclusionary hous-ing programs in California, Schwartz and Johnson (1983) note that "There is no substitute for basic development policies that provide a suit-able supply of vacant land zoned for housing at a wide variety of densi-ties, permit subdivisions of lots at appropriate rates, and do not persis-tently restrict the rate of building permit approval below demand." Research for this report indicates overwhelmingly that density bonuses and regulatory waivers, in and of themselves, do not lead to the creation of affordable housing units. Such techniques are used most effectively in concert with direct subsidies and where there is adequate land zoned to accommodate housing of all types and for all income groups.

This section of the report addresses the inclusionary techniques that are considered incentives per se (i.e., bonuses and waivers). Other mecha-nisms (e.g., mandatory set-asides, fee-in-lieu programs) are referenced here only in the context that they relate to incentive provisions. State re-quirements for local housing planning are also discussed here because the jurisdictions that are considered to have had success with such housing programs are by and large in states that mandate local governments to use such techniques.

Mandatory set-asides require that residential developments over a cer-tain size include a prescribed percentage of units for low- and moderate-income households. Under some ordinances, set-asides may only be re-quired where federal and state housing subsidies are available for the lower-income units or if a public housing authority plans to acquire or lease them (Mandelker 1997, Section 7.26). Density bonuses are some-times offered with mandatory set-asides. Bonuses are granted to develop-ers wherein each unit of affordable housing provided is equated with an added number of dwelling units permitted to be sold or rented at market rate. Some ordinances scale the density bonuses according to certain af-fordability ranges (i.e., greater bonuses are offered for the provisions of the most needed or difficult-to-provide housing for target populations). Where there are not subsidies available, density bonuses may be com-bined with set-asides to help defray the losses incurred by the developer on the lower-income units.

Additional incentives are provided to developers in the form of waivers or reductions in site development standards or modifications of zoning code requirements or architectural design requirements. These include re-ductions in setback, floor area, and off-street parking requirements. Inclusionary ordinances also often contain alternative means for develop-ers to meet the intent of law (e.g., making payments to a housing trust fund in lieu of actually constructing the housing, providing the housing off site, or dedicating land to the jurisdiction on which such housing will be built by a public or nonprofit entity).

CALIFORNIA

California enacted legislation in 1989 (California Government Code, Section 65915) requiring local governments to prepare a housing plan el-ement and provide density bonuses and other incentives and concessions to developers of affordable housing. The impetus for the legislation was a housing shortage for low- and moderate-income families and ever-in-creasing housing costs brought on by skyrocketing real estate values in the 1970s and 1980s. Local government permitting processes and land-use regulations aimed at slowing or managing growth were also factors (Calavita and Grimes 1998). The California program has been described as "decentralized, flexible, ad hoc, diverse and complex, as it reflects the political, economic and cultural traits of each locality over time" (Calavita and Grimes 1998, 164). The political aspect of this description refers to differing philosophies among governors and their administrations between the 1970s and 1990s regarding both the causes of the affordable housing shortage and the appropriate level of government intervention to solve the problem. The result of this ongoing debate has been that, although local governments are mandated to adhere to certain inclusionary housing requirements, most local governments that have had any success in getting housing produced have crafted their own solutions, using the state requirements more as a framework that an absolute plan. Petaluma and San Jose, described below, are two such communities. The downside to the fluctuating message from the state regarding this issue has been that many communities have merely adopted housing plan elements and inclusionary housing ordinances, but have not implemented them.

The housing legislation requires local governments to first prepare a housing plan element as part of a general plan and to subsequently provide density bonuses in order to meet their affordable housing goals. The housing element must consist of "an analysis of existing and projected housing needs and a statement of goals, policies, quantified objectives, financial resources, and scheduled programs for the preservation, improvement, and development of housing" (Section 65583). The element must also outline the actions the local government will undertake to implement the housing element, including land-use and development controls, regulatory concessions and incentives, and the use of federal and state financing and subsidy programs.

Local governments are also required by state statute to provide incentives—in the form of density bonuses and regulatory waivers—to developers who build affordable housing (Section 65915). The law provides that local governments shall grant density bonuses of at least 25 percent, plus an additional incentive or equivalent financial incentive, to housing developers who agree to construct at least: 20 percent of the units affordable to lower-income households, 10 percent of the units affordable to very-low-income households, or senior citizen housing. The law also requires local governments to establish procedures to waive or modify "development and zoning standards which would otherwise inhibit the utilization of the density bonus on specific sites. These procedures shall include, but not be limited to, such items as minimum lot size, side yard setbacks, and placement of public works improvements."

The most recent figures available show that, as of 1992, 26 California counties (out of 58) and 196 municipalities (out of 474) had enacted density bonus ordinances (Office of Planning Research 1992).

The other incentives and concessions that local governments may provide include:

- a reduction in setback and square-footage requirements;

- a reduction in parking requirements;

- approval of mixed-use zoning; and

- other regulatory incentives or concessions that a developer or the city may propose for which "identifiable cost reductions" can be shown.

To implement the density bonuses, the statute enables local governments to require developers to enter into a development agreement. Such an agreement would stipulate the exact terms of the bonuses the developer would receive and the incentives and concession made by the local government. Finally, the law directs courts to uphold the decision of a city or county, or to grant the density bonus if it finds that the bonus will as-

California's housing legislation requires local governments to first prepare a housing plan element as part of a general plan and to subsequently provide density bonuses in order to meet their affordable housing goals. . . . Local governments are also required by state statute to provide incentives—in the form of density bonuses and regulatory waivers—to developers who build affordable housing.

sist the local government in meeting its share of the regional housing needs or in implementing its congestion management plan.

Finally, the California Community Redevelopment Law is also instrumental in getting affordable housing units built in areas where that law is being applied. Under the redevelopment law, 20 percent of the revenues generated in locally designated redevelopment areas must be used to increase or improve housing for low- and moderate-income households (Section 33334.2). Local redevelopment agencies are further required to ensure that at least 30 percent of all the new or rehabilitated units it develops are affordable to low- and moderate-income persons, with no less than half of those units affordable to persons of very low income. Only half of those new units have to be in the redevelopment area (Section 33413(b)). Within redevelopment areas, 15 percent of all private and public units must be affordable. In fiscal year 1994-1995, there were 5,037 affordable units produced under the 30 percent requirement and 251 units under the 15 percent requirement (Calavita and Grimes 1998).

According to Linda Wheaton, housing policy specialist with the California Department of Housing and Community Development, the most common use of the density bonuses is for assisted rental housing (Wheaton 1999). The bonuses are used less often for for-sale residential developments because the statute requires that they remain affordable for 10 to 30 years. Such a requirement provides no opportunity for equity recapture on the part of first-time home buyers. Thus, says Wheaton, the requirements aimed at keeping housing units affordable are not reconciled with overarching goals helping families build equity and financial stability through home ownership. Finally, in terms of regulatory concessions, Wheaton says the most common waiver offered by local governments and sought out by developers is the reduction in parking requirements.

As mentioned above, two California cities, Petaluma and San Jose, that have been recognized for having effective affordable housing programs, rely far more on locally crafted solutions than state directives to meet housing goals. These solutions have involved direct subsidies (with money generated through the state redevelopment law) and leveraging.

The city of Petaluma, California, is recognized as having one of the most successful affordable housing programs in California (Amoroso 2000). Between 1990 and 1999, the city financed more than 100 new affordable housing units annually. Bonnie Gaebler, the city's housing administrator, says that density bonuses and regulatory waivers may "sweeten the pot" for developers of affordable housing but, in the absence of financial subsidies, "would not result in a single unit of affordable housing getting built" (Gaebler 2000). In addition to money, the other key to the city's success she says is the "longstanding, unwavering commitment" of the Petaluma City Council to providing housing for all residents, from homeless single persons to first-time home buyers. Gaebler notes that the regional housing needs determination assigned to Petaluma is far below what will be needed in that city, given the city's job creation projection.

The city has a housing trust fund that is financed by tax increment revenues in designated redevelopment areas, Community Development Block Grant monies, and developer contributions in lieu of building affordable housing. The fund is used to leverage private and nonprofit investments in affordable housing. It also is used to pay for impact fees for affordable housing units in developments where 10 to15 percent of the units have been set aside for low-income or very-low-income households. As such, affordable housing projects are not necessarily excused from all impact or permit fees, but, rather than coming out of the developer's pocket or being passed on to the home buyer, there is a transfer of city funds from one account to another. Gaebler says the fact that affordable housing developments pay their own way, albeit indirectly, helps relieve political pressure against them.

A similar scenario exists on the opposite end of the Bay Area in San Jose. That city's success with regard to affordable housing is attributable to outright land acquisition, leveraged private investment using revenue generated through property tax increments in the city's redevelopment planning areas, and a flexible approach to accommodating housing development wherever possible says Kent Edens, Deputy Director or Planning (Edens 2000). San Jose generates approximately $20 million per year for affordable housing through the tax increment mechanism. The city's housing agency uses that money to leverage approximately seven times that amount in private investment.

The San Jose 2020 General Plan serves as the "definitive" guide to land development in the city and has several mechanisms built in to encourage housing development. Adopted in 1994, it is the city's first modern plan that meets the various requirements of state law, if not the exact letter of the law, says Edens. To start, the plan designates a substantial amount of land for housing development. Further, it contains "Discretionary Alternate Use Policies" that allow various commercial or industrial sites to be redeveloped as housing at the discretion of the city council. For example, sites along major commercial streets and around future light rail stations may be redeveloped as high-density housing if a proposal meets the goals and policies of the General Plan. Most development in San Jose takes place through Planned Residential District zoning, which provides the city and developers with a lot of flexibility as to where housing may be built, but gives the city council substantial control in implementing housing goals overall. Finally, the city does provide density bonuses. Zoned densities of 12 to 25 dwelling units per acre may be increased to 25 to 40 dwelling units per acre if 100 percent of the units in the project are affordable. Similar bonuses are available for projects that contain all rental units.

Edens says the city has more than met the intent of the state-mandated housing element and exceeded its allocated Regional Housing Needs Determination assigned to it by the Association of Bay Area Governments.

NEW JERSEY

The statewide inclusionary housing program in New Jersey was born out of two significant state Supreme Court decisions regarding an exclusionary zoning ordinance in the Philadelphia suburb of Mt. Laurel. In the first Mt. Laurel decision (*South Burlington County NAACP v. Mount Laurel*, 67 N.J. 151, A.2d 713 (1975), *cert. denied*, 423 U.S. 808 (1975)), the N.J. Supreme Court established a constitutional obligation for each of the 566 municipalities in the state to use zoning and land-use powers to establish a realistic opportunity for the provision of its fair-share, low- and moderate-income housing obligations. In *Mt. Laurel I*, the court's decision established a "builder's remedy." Consequently, when a developer sued a municipality for exclusionary zoning practices, the municipality would have been ordered by the court to allow, for example, four market-rate units for every unit of affordable housing built. Essentially the builder would go to court to get the building permit. Following the second Mount Laurel ruling, known as *Mt. Laurel II* (92 N.J. 158, 456 A.2d 390 (1983)), more options were introduced for how each municipality could reach its constitutional obligation. *Mt. Laurel II* led to the passage of the Fair

These homes in Washington Township in Mercer County are the result of New Jersey's provisions for its fair-share, low- and moderate-income housing program.

In Wall Township in Monmouth County, New Jersey, the affordable housing initiative has used infill housing to create more affordable housing opportunities.

Housing Act and the formation of the Council on Affordable Housing (COAH), which the state charged with implementing the fair-share doctrine and now serves as an administrative alternative to the court system. *Mt. Laurel II* approved and required affirmative governmental actions to meet the fair-share obligation, including the use of density bonuses and mandatory set-asides (Mandelker 1997).

The New Jersey Fair Housing Act (New Jersey Statutes Annotated, Section 52:27 D-310) provides municipalities with the option of preparing a housing element for their general plans and describes the essential components of such elements. The housing element must include:

- an inventory of existing housing stock and a projection of probable future construction of new affordable housing units;

- an analysis of demographic and income trends and incomes;

- employment projections;

- a determination of the municipality's present and prospective fair share for low- and moderate-income housing;

- the municipality's capacity to accommodate its present and prospective housing needs, including its fair share of low- and moderate-income housing; and

- a consideration of the lands within the jurisdiction that are appropriate for construction of affordable housing as well as analysis of existing structures that may be appropriate for conversion to affordable housing.

The Fair Housing Act enables a municipality to provide for its fair share of low- and moderate-income housing "by means of any technique or combination of techniques which provide a realistic opportunity for the provision of the fair share." In preparing the housing element, municipalities are to consider eight types of techniques.

1) Rezoning for densities necessary to ensure the economic viability of any inclusionary developments, either through mandatory set-asides or density bonuses, as may be necessary to meet all or part of the municipality's fair share

2) Determination of the total residential zoning necessary to ensure that the municipality's fair share is achieved

3) Determination of measures that the municipality will take to ensure that low- and moderate-income units remain affordable to low- and moderate-income households for a period of not less than six years

4) A plan for infrastructure expansion and rehabilitation if necessary to ensure the achievement of the municipality's fair-share goal for low- and moderate-income housing

5) Donation or use of municipally owned land or land condemned by the municipality for purposes of providing low- and moderate-income housing

6) Tax abatements for the purpose of providing low- and moderate-income housing

7) Use of funds obtained from any state or federal subsidy toward the construction of low- and moderate-income housing

8) Use of municipally generated funds toward the construction of low- and moderate-income housing

New Jersey municipalities enter the COAH process voluntarily by filing the housing element described above, which must include a fair-share plan establishing how the municipality will provide for a number of units affordable to low- and moderate-income households. The municipalities' fair share is predetermined by COAH using a computation formula that establishes the number of new and rehabilitated units of affordable housing that must be accommodated in each housing region across the state and within each municipality. The formula is based on projections of economic growth and development likely to occur in the region.

Within two years of filing its housing plan, a municipality must petition COAH for substantive certification (i.e., approval) of the plan if a municipality is to remain under COAH's jurisdiction. Petitioning protects the municipality from lawsuits while COAH reviews the housing element. Certification is granted for a six-year period and may be withdrawn if a municipality fails to provide a "realistic opportunity" to fulfill its fair-share housing obligation.

Municipalities that do not participate in the process are not shielded from lawsuits. Cases in which a developer has had repeated difficulty getting a housing development approved are referred to COAH, which can do one of two things. For site-specific issues, it can directly prescribe a permitted density on which the developer will provide affordable housing as part of a larger development (similar to how the builder's remedy was used prior to *Mt. Laurel II*). Or COAH can negotiate a settlement between the developer and the municipality as to how the housing will be accommodated within the municipality or through a regional contribution agreement.

New Jersey municipalities enter the COAH process voluntarily by filing the housing element described above, which must include a fair-share plan establishing how the municipality will provide for a number of units affordable to low- and moderate-income households.

This house provides a five-bedroom group home for seniors of low and moderate income in Bridgewater, New Jersey.

Council on Affordable Housing

As of June 1998, 41 percent of New Jersey's 566 municipalities were participating in the COAH process (www.state.nj.us/dca/coah); that is, they have submitted a housing element and fair-share plan to COAH, which has certified it or is in the process of doing so. The most common technique used by municipalities to implement the housing plan is to rezone lands at higher density levels than what is typically allowed to create realistic opportunities for affordable housing to be developed (Slachetka 2000). Another common technique is an affordable housing overlay zone through which local governments permit affordable housing development in underused industrial areas in order to capture housing opportunities. This is especially common in cities that have a shortage of vacant land available for affordable housing.

An additional incentive for municipalities to enter the COAH certification process is that they can then levy development fees on market-rate residential development and nonresidential development. Monies raised from the fees are deposited into a housing trust fund. The New Jersey Supreme Court, in *Holmdel Builder's Ass'n. v. Holmdel Township*, 121 N.J. 550 (1990) determined that mandatory development fees are both statutorily and constitutionally permissible. COAH reviews and approves all local development fee ordinances and the accompanying spending plans.

As of June 1999, 97 municipalities had enacted development fee ordinances, and 84 of them had COAH-approved spending plans. A total of $74 million in fees had been collected by that time. Brick Township, for example, has collected more than $1 million, which is earmarked for low-interest loans and closing costs, rehabilitation, new single-family infill construction, and senior housing (New Jersey Council on Affordable Housing 1999). Local governments may impose fees of no more than one-half of 1 percent of the equalized assessed value of residential development and up to 1 percent of equalized assessed value for nonresidential development. In specified districts, the local government may provide density bonuses through rezoning. In such areas, the local government may impose development fees of up to 6 percent of the equalized value of the additional market-rate residential units generated through the density bonus. Developers are exempt from paying development fees on affordable housing units.

The Fair Housing Act also permits municipalities with COAH-certified plans (as well as those under court order to comply) to transfer up to 50 percent of their fair-share obligations to one or more municipalities within the applicable housing region. Such arrangements are called regional contribution agreements (RCAs).

The Fair Housing Act also permits municipalities with COAH-certified plans (as well as those under court order to comply) to transfer up to 50 percent of their fair-share obligations to one or more municipalities within the applicable housing region. Such arrangements are called regional contribution agreements (RCAs). The sending municipality must transfer a negotiated payment now established at $20,000 per unit as the minimum. Funds may be used by receiving municipalities to subsidize new construction or to rehabilitate existing units for occupancy by low- or moderate-income households. There are 22 municipalities acting as receiving areas under RCAs (www.state.nj.us/dca/coah). Almost $150 million has been transferred into these areas through the RCAs (Slachetka 2000).

Under certain conditions, a municipality's fair-share allocation may be adjusted downward by COAH. Generally, this is done if implementation of the fair-share allocation would violate other community planning objectives or if the municipality has a shortage of vacant and developable land. Considerations include the potential impact on infrastructure, historic preservation, environmentally sensitive lands, farmland and open space preservation, and an established pattern of development. These considerations are intended to ensure that the affordable housing program is integrated into the municipality's comprehensive planning process and that it is consistent with the designated planning areas in the State Development and Redevelopment Plan (Sections 1 through 12 of Public Law 1985, c.398 (C.52:18A-196 et seq.)). The Planning Areas are: PA1: Metropolitan Planning Area; PA2: Suburban Planning Area; PA3: Fringe Planning Area; PA4: Rural Planning Area, which includes PA4B, the Rural/Environmentally Sensitive Planning Area; and PA5: Environmentally Sensitive Planning Area, which includes PA5B, the Environmentally Sensitive/Barrier Island Planning Area.

These planning areas reflect distinct geographic and economic units within the state and serve as an organizing framework for application of the statewide policies of the state plan. Within each of the planning areas, municipalities designate "centers," which are areas that include already urbanized uses and into which additional development (ideally in compact patterns at higher density than what would normally exist in the absence of a state planning process), is directed. Much of the housing obligation that is transferred via RCAs is directed into these centers. This helps meet the objectives of the state plan in terms of stemming sprawl, results in direct investment in areas that might otherwise not experience it, and fulfills affordable housing goals for the sending and receiving municipalities.

OREGON

The Oregon inclusionary housing program uses the statewide land-use planning program to ensure that each municipality provides an adequate supply of land for housing of all types.

Goal 10 of Oregon's statewide planning program on housing calls for local governments to encourage the availability of adequate housing at prices and rents affordable to Oregon households. Goal 14 on urbanization requires local governments to adopt urban growth boundaries that contain land sufficient to accommodate projected growth, which includes growth in the need for affordable housing. (A complete description of the Oregon Statewide Land Use Program and the 19 Statewide Goals is available at www.lcd.state.or.us/.)

The state Land Conservation and Development Commission (LCDC) reviews local plans and land-use regulations to ensure that the plans comply with state goals. In *Seaman v. City of Durham*, LCDC No. 770925(1978), the commission held that the state housing goal incorporates the *Mt. Laurel* fair-share doctrine. The state legislation (Oregon Revised Statutes, Section 197.296(b)(3)) to implement the fair-share policy describes the housing needs analysis that local governments must undertake when they periodically review and amend their urban growth boundaries. If the analysis reveals that sufficient land does not exist to accommodate af-

Under certain conditions, a municipality's fair-share allocation may be adjusted downward by COAH. . . . Considerations include the potential impact on infrastructure, historic preservation, environmentally sensitive lands, farmland and open space preservation, and an established pattern of development. These considerations are intended to ensure that the affordable housing program is integrated into the municipality's comprehensive planning process. . . .

fordable housing, the statute provides local governments with several options. It may:

- amend the urban growth boundary;

- amend its comprehensive plan or land-use regulations to include new measures to increase the likelihood that residential development will occur at densities sufficient to accommodate housing needs for 20 years without expansion of the urban growth boundary (Section 197.296(4)); and

- undertake additional actions or measures to ensure that sufficient buildable land exists, including:

    (a) increases in the permitted density on existing residential land;

    (b) financial incentives for higher-density housing;

    (c) provisions permitting additional density beyond that generally allowed in the zoning district in exchange for amenities and features provided by the developer;

    (d) removal or easing of approval standards or procedures;

    (e) minimum density ranges;

    (f) redevelopment and infill strategies;

    (g) authorization of housing types not previously allowed by the plan or regulations; and

    (h) adoption of an average residential density standard (Section 197.297(7)).

In the Portland metropolitan area, Goal 10 is supplemented with an administrative rule adopted by LCDC that specifies overall average density objectives, ranging from 6 to 10 units per acre, for each of the cities and urban portions of the three counties that make up the region (Oregon Administrative Rules 660-007-0035). Moreover, the rule requires most of the cities in the region to "provide for the opportunity for at least 50 percent of new residential units to be attached single-family housing or multiple-family housing" (Oregon Administrative Rules 660-007-0030).

In the Portland metropolitan area, 50 percent of new residential units must be attached single-family housing or multiple-family housing, such as these row houses on Killingsworth Avenue in the Sabin neighborhood of Northeast Portland.

Marya Morris

Marya Morris

The City of Portland has an extensive set of programs to encourage affordable housing and meet the goals set by the fair-share plan for the region. In response to a 1999 survey by Portland Metro on affordable housing tools, the city of Portland listed seven primary and 38 total regulatory and financial techniques that it currently uses to promote affordable housing.

Mike Saba of the Portland Planning Bureau says that, while regulatory tools are useful in making projects more feasible and support innovative projects, direct or indirect funding (e.g., property tax relief), either upfront or ongoing, is far more effective in producing tangible results (Saba 2000).

According to a 1997 assessment of the entire Oregon statewide planning process, "Oregon's land use laws have had a significant, if unheralded, impact in sharply increasing the amount of land zoned for more affordable types of housing from apartment build-

Center Commons is a high-density, affordable housing development in Northeast Portland. It meets both the city and Metro governments' goals to provide affordable housing on infill sites that are accessible by public transit. The MAX light rail station is visible to the right of the building shown below.

Marya Morris

ings to manufactured housing" (1000 Friends 1997,19). Even with this glowing assessment, the study gave the state an overall grade of "B" in meeting statewide housing objectives, indicating that projected population growth will require even more affordable housing to be built than current projections have planned for. Additional progress could be made by permitting accessory dwelling units in single-family zones, adopting inclusionary zoning (specifically mandatory set-asides), and setting firm minimum densities that encourage compact, affordable development.

Despite the report's recommendations for increased use in mandatory set-asides, Oregon Governor Kitzhaber signed a bill in June 1999 (HB 2658) that expressly prohibits local governments from adopting regulations, or imposing as a condition for development approval, a requirement that has the effect of establishing the sales price for a housing unit or that requires a housing unit to be designated for sale to any particular class or group of purchasers. Such provisions are typical in mandatory set-aside requirements. The act also states, however, that it is not intended to limit the authority of local governments to implement incentives, contract commitments, density bonuses, or other voluntary regulations, provisions, or conditions designed to increase the supply of moderate- or lower-cost housing units.

With HB 2658 effectively prohibiting mandatory inclusionary housing programs in Oregon, the Portland Metro Regional Affordable Housing Strategy, the housing plan adopted in June 2000 by the Metro government, recommended that the agency instead implement a voluntary regionwide inclusionary housing program (among many other tools). As part of the program, Metro will prepare a model ordinance and a set of best practice guides for use by location jurisdictions. The strategy also contains a recommendation to tie inclusionary housing requirements to a regional housing funding source and to recognize affordable housing as a "special land need" for which the urban growth boundary could be amended.

The regional strategy further recommends that local governments enact voluntary inclusionary housing programs as well as some creative zoning techniques that can help make affordable housing feasible, including minimum densities, maximum square-footage limits, single-car garage requirements, and minimum percentages for land zoned for multifamily housing.

FLORIDA

Similar to the way that California, New Jersey, and Oregon address housing affordability issues, the state of Florida requires local governments to prepare a housing element in the local comprehensive plan. The state comprehensive plan also contains a housing goal and calls on the public and private sectors to "increase the affordability of housing for low-income and moderate-income persons" (Florida Statutes, Section 187.201(5)(a)). The local housing element must contain a housing needs analysis and set forth standards and plans for providing housing for all existing and projected future residents and "adequate sites for future housing for low-income and moderate-income families" (Section 163.3177(6)(f)). State law expressly enables local governments to "encourage the use of innovative land development regulations which include provisions such as transfer of development rights, incentive and inclusionary zoning, planned-unit development, impact fees, and performance zoning" (Section 163.33202(3)).

In addition to the housing element, local governments must prepare a local housing assistance plan to be eligible to participate in the State

Housing Initiatives Partnership Program (SHIPP), which is Florida's statewide housing trust fund. The housing assistance plans are intended to increase the availability of affordable residential units by combining local resources and cost-saving measures into a local housing partnership and using private and public funds to reduce the cost of housing (Section 420.9075). Specifically, SHIPP funds are available to create local housing partnerships, to expand production of and preserve affordable housing, and to increase housing-related employment (Section 420.9072).

Florida's housing statute defines local housing incentives broadly to include expedited permitting procedures, ongoing review of local policies and ordinances to ensure that housing costs are minimized, and "other regulatory reforms" (Section 420.9071 (16)). The reforms that local governments may implement include:

- modification, reduction, or waivers of impact fees;

- modification of street standards;

- allowance of increased density, zero lot line configurations, and accessory apartments; and

- reduction of parking and setback requirements (Section 420.9076 (4)).

A unique provision in the Florida statute includes mandates that each municipality prepare a printed inventory of locally owned public land suitable for affordable housing (Section 420.9076 (4)(j)).

The city of Orlando has provisions for regulatory incentives and density bonuses for affordable housing (as well as for urban design features in the downtown). The regulatory incentive programs are intended to implement the housing objectives of the city's growth management plan by providing alternative development standards in the form of flexible design options that "incorporate cost saving measures without compromising the quality of the resulting development" (Orlando Code, Section 67.601).

Developers who wish to take advantage of the alternative development standards are required to have their development application certified as an affordable housing project by the city. Once a project is certified, the developer may be eligible for relaxation of certain site development standards, such as lot coverage and setback standards. According to Orlando housing planner Frances DeJesus, the most important provision is that developers are reimbursed for 100 percent of the road and sewer impact fees, and receive a 62 percent discount on school impact fees for housing units in certified affordable housing developments. Funds to pay for the reimbursements come directly from the city's general revenue fund.

Developers of market-rate housing may qualify for a density bonus in exchange for a financial contribution to the city's local housing trust fund (Orlando Code, Section 67.302(14)). This provision is rarely used, according to DeJesus, who says that zoned densities in the city of Orlando are high enough that developers generally are not looking for ways to add density.

As is the case with the California cities described above, density bonuses and regulatory waivers for affordable housing are "one piece of the puzzle" in making housing affordable, says DeJesus. These tools are only effective, she says, when coupled with direct financial incentives provided through the state housing investment program, such as construction loans and down payment assistance.

As is the case with the California cities described above, density bonuses and regulatory waivers for affordable housing are "one piece of the puzzle" in making housing affordable in Orlando, says DeJesus. These tools are only effective, she says, when coupled with direct financial incentives provided through the state housing investment program, such as construction loans and down payment assistance.

The Montgomery County, Maryland, affordable housing program is regarded by many as the most successful one of its kind in the country. Because affordable housing is provided in every new subdivision in the county, the program has also been credited with creating neighborhoods of mixed income and race. (Above) A duplex containing two MPDUs in the Clagget Farm subdivision. (Below) A market-rate, single-family home with similar appearance to the MPDU duplex, also in Clagget Farm subdivision.

MONTGOMERY COUNTY, MARYLAND

The Montgomery County, Maryland, affordable housing program is regarded by many as the most successful one of its kind in the country. Since 1974, the county's Moderately Priced Dwelling Unit (MPDU) program, which combines mandatory set-asides and density bonuses, has produced approximately 10,000 dwelling units (Montgomery County Code Chapter 25A). By contrast, New Jersey's statewide fair-share program has produced 23,000 units (some of which have yet to be built). In California, 75 municipalities that have implemented the density bonus program have collectively produced 25,000 units since the early 1980s (Swope 2000). Because affordable housing is provided in every new subdivision in the county, the program has also been credited with creating neighborhoods of mixed income and race.

The program was adopted as part of the county zoning legislation and is managed by the county department of housing and community development. Certain program requirements, such as income limits, maximum sales prices, and rental rates, are set through executive regulations that are developed by the department staff and approved by the county council and the county executive. (For more information, consult the program's web site, www.co.mo.md.us/services/hca/Housing/MPDU/mpdu.htm).

Montgomery County Department of Housing and Community Affairs

A typical MPDU is a three-bedroom, bath-and-a-half townhome, such as this one in the Potomac Regency subdivision of North Bethesda.

The program requires that 12.5 to 15 percent of all housing units in residential developments of 50 units or more be priced affordably. In exchange, the developer is allowed to build up to 22 percent more units than the zoning would otherwise permit. The program serves both moderate-income homebuyers and renters and low-income renters. In the first category, moderate-income households (i.e., those whose incomes are 65 percent of the median for the county) are able to purchase or rent housing at a below-market rate. In 1997, the average income of an MPDU purchaser was $29,014, and the average MPDU sold for $90,180 (Swope 2000). According to the county's web site, MPDUs range in price from $60,000 for a one-bedroom condominium to approximately $110,000 for a three-bedroom detached house with a basement and garage (www.co. mo.md.us/services/hca/Housing/MPDU/summary.htm). The units that are sold are price-controlled for 10 years.

The second category is aimed at low-income renters. One-third of the affordable units provided by developers are set aside for purchase by the county's Housing Opportunities Commission (the county's public housing authority) or nonprofit groups, which in turn rent the units to low-income households. The income of tenants who rent these units ranges from below $10,000 to $36,150. As of May 2000, HOC owns 1,600 housing units, and nonprofit housing sponsors have purchased about 65 units.

The program's two most commonly noted achievements are the high number of units provided over the last three decades and the economic and racial integration of suburban neighborhoods. These achievements are also the root of the most common criticisms and limitations of the program, the first of which is that the program is too dependent on sustained long-term growth. The success of the program has been the direct result of a favorable housing market in which there has been high demand for market-rate units. When the economy slowed down in the early 1990s, for example, fewer than 350 units of affordable housing were provided, enough to provide housing for just 20 percent of households on the waiting list. This scenario is similar to the urban design bonus program in Hartford, Connecticut, described in Part 2, where there has been no downtown development project large enough since the 1980s that would trigger the bonus program, thus no street-level amenities have been provided.

And while the healthy housing market helped meet Montgomery County's housing goals for all income levels, it also fueled urban sprawl and put pressure on county roads, sewers, and schools. The rapid growth and high residential densities resulting from the program have brought criticism from slow growth or no-growth advocates who are concerned about the county's ability to provide adequate services for all residents.

Maryland's smart growth program, enacted in 1992 and expanded in 1997, adds another wrinkle to the scenario. In the state's effort to stem sprawl and urbanization of the remaining undeveloped areas in the state, cities and counties have been directed to draw Priority Funding Areas where growth will be directed and into which state monies that support growth will be channeled. In large part, housing built under the affordable housing program has been on greenfield sites on the urban fringe, in the types of areas where growth will now be discouraged as the state tries to get a handle on urban sprawl. Using state spending on schools, roads, and other infrastructure as an incentive, much of the new growth that is projected in the state in the coming decades will be within city and county designated Priority Funding Areas. Aside from the growth management issue, the county may be running out of land for large projects anyway; much of the land zoned for one-half acre and smaller lots has already been developed, therefore fewer subdivisions of 50 or more units will be submitted for development approval in the future.

Another common criticism has been that the mix of race and income in the suburbs that results from the mandatory set-aside is a form of social engineering. Supporters of the program, such as urban theorist and former Albuquerque mayor David Rusk, have noted that the program is in fact an antidote to the "purest form" of social engineering—namely, exclusionary zoning (Walljasper 1999).

In the coming decades, the county will have to address both the dwindling supply of affordable units as the 10-year price controls on those units expire as well as the loss of rental housing to conversion to market-rate, upscale condominiums. These changes, coupled with dwindling land supply and the state's emphasis on compact development, will likely mean a change of strategy for the county.

CONCLUSIONS

Analyzing inclusionary housing legislation for the purpose of identifying best local practices or creating model legislation raises as many questions as it does answers. What is clear from looking at the most extensive state programs is that provision of density bonuses and regulatory waivers of fees or development standards—while two of the most common tools used to implement mandatory housing plans—are not sufficient incentives in and of themselves to get developers to build affordable housing. What does work are carefully crafted packages of financial and regulatory techniques that remove barriers to affordable housing but also meet the overall community planning objectives.

What is less clear is the appropriate role of state government in overseeing such programs and in promulgating standards. Planners in San Jose and Petaluma concurred that, at times, state requirements, such as the mandatory implementation of a density bonus ordinance, may create more work for local governments than is necessary and not be an effective technique for getting housing built. Moreover, the regional housing needs determination, which is the number of units that the regional agencies assign to each governments of its "fair share" of affordable housing, may be alternately too low or too high given population and employment projections. The latter situation has occurred in New Jersey, where the state Council on Affordable Housing has had to issue rules describing the myriad conditions under which a local government may lower its regional fair-share requirement so that it is tailored to local conditions regarding buildable land, employment projections, and other factors.

That said, the cities of Petaluma and San Jose are rare exceptions to the rule—communities whose residents and elected officials have made an ongoing commitment to providing affordable housing. In other communities where regulatory barriers are the norm and little effort is expended in accommodating all housing types, it would seem that mandating a housing element and the use of these tools is the only method for solving the problem, short of a steady stream of litigation.

1000 Friends of Oregon. 1997. "Housing Affordability: Grade B." *Landmark* (February): 19.

Amoroso, Alex. 1999. Housing Planner, Association of Bay Area Governments, Oakland, Calif. Telephone interview. 20 December.

Arlington County, Virginia. 1992. *Rosslyn Area Plan Addendum.* Arlington, Va.

Benner, Richard. 1978. "Housing Affordability by Design." *Oregon's Future* (Fall): 26-30.

Benson, David J. 1970. "Bonus or Incentive Zoning—Legal Implications." *Syracuse Law Review* 21: 895.

Bernick, Michael, and Robert Cervero. 1997. *Transit Villages in the 21st Century.* New York: McGraw Hill.

Brooks, Mary. 1970. *Bonus Provisions in Central City Areas.* Planning Advisory Service Report 257. Chicago: American Planning Association.

Calavita, Nico, and Kenneth Grimes. 1998. "Inclusionary Housing in California: The Experience of Two Decades." *Journal of the American Planning Association* 64, no. 2: 150-69.

Callies, David L., Robert H. Freilich, and Thomas E. Roberts. 1999. *Cases and Materials on Land Use.* 3d ed. St. Paul, Minn.: The West Group.

Chicago, City of. Department of Planning and Development. 2000. *A New Zoning Bonus System for Chicago.* Public Review Draft. July.

Craswell, Cathy. 1996. Model Density Bonus Ordinance. Memorandum to [California] Planning Directors and Other Interested Parties. Sacramento: California Department of Housing and Community Development, Housing Policy Development Division. 6 August.

DeJesus, Frances. 2000. Planner, City of Orlando, Florida, Department of Housing and Community Development. Telephone interview. 18 January.

Denny Triangle Neighborhood Planning Committee. 1998. *Denny Triangle Neighborhood Plan.* Seattle, Washington.

Edens, Kent. 2000. Deputy Director of Planning, City of San Jose, California. Telephone interview. 14 January.

Gaebler, Bonnie. 2000. Housing Administrator, City of Petaluma, California. Telephone interview. 11 January.

Getzels, Judith, and Martin Jaffe, with Brian W. Blaesser and Robert F. Brown. 1988. *Zoning Bonuses in Central Cities.* Planning Advisory Service Report No. 410. Chicago: American Planning Association.

Heyman, I. Michael. 1970. "Innovative Land Regulation and Comprehensive Planning." In *The New Zoning: Legal, Administrative, and Economic Concepts and Techniques,*, edited by Norman Marcus and Marilyn Groves. New York: Praeger Publishers.

Johnston, Robert A., Seymour Schwartz, Geoffrey A. Wandesforde-Smith, and Michael Caplan. 1990. "Selling Zoning: Do Density Bonus Incentives for Moderate Cost Housing Work?" *Land Use Law & Zoning Digest* (August): 3-9.

Kayden, Jerold S. 1978. *Incentive Zoning in New York City: A Cost-Benefit Analysis.* Cambridge, Mass.: Lincoln Land Institute of Land Policy.

_____. 1992. "Market-Based Regulatory Approaches: A Comparative Discussion of Environmental and Land Use Techniques in the United States." *Boston College Environmental Affairs Law Review* 19: 565.

_____. 1999. Unpublished proceedings of Doris Duke Foundation symposium on compensatory regulations, Chicago, Illinois, 17 September.

_____. 2000. "Plaza Suit." *Planning* (March): 16–19.

_____. Forthcoming. *Privately Owned Public Spaces.* New York: John Wiley and sons.

Klee, Roland. 1999. Principal Planner, City of Hartford, Connecticut. Telephone interview. 22 October.

Knaap, Gerrit J. 1990. "State Land Use Planning and Inclusionary Zoning: Evidence from Oregon." *Journal of Planning Education and Research* 10, no. 1: 39-46.

Lassar, Terry Jill. 1989. *Carrots & Sticks: New Zoning Downtown*. Washington, D.C.: The Urban Land Institute.

Mallach, Alan. 1984. *Inclusionary Housing Programs: Policies and Practices*. New Brunswick, N.J.: Rutgers University.

Mandelker, Daniel R. 1970. "The Basic Philosophy of Zoning: Incentive or Restraint?" In *The New Zoning: Legal, Administrative, and Economic Concepts and Techniques*, edited by Norman Marcus and Marilyn W. Groves. New York: Praeger.

_____. 1997. *Land Use Law*. 4th ed. Charlottesville, Va.: Lexus Law Publishing.

Meshenberg, Michael. 1976. *The Administration of Flexible Zoning Techniques*. Planning Advisory Service Report No. 318. Chicago: American Planning Association.

Minneapolis, City of. *The Minneapolis Plan*. (Available at www.ci.minneapolis. mn.us/citywork/planning/planpubs/mplsplan)

Morgan, Jennifer. "Zoning for All: Using Inclusionary Zoning Techniques to Promote Affordable Housing." *Emory Law Journal* 44 (Winter 1995): 359.

National Commission on Urban Problems (Douglas Commission). 1968. *Building the American City*. Washington, D.C.: U.S. Government Printing Office.

New Jersey Council on Affordable Housing. 1999. *Designing Affordable Housing. The 1998-1999 Annual Report*. Trenton, N.J.

New York City Planning Department. 1999. Unified Bulk Program. Executive Summary. December 8. (Available at: www.ci.nyc.ny.us/html/dcp/html/bulksum.html)

Newman, Richard A., and Phil T. Feola. 1989. "Housing Incentives, A National Perspective." *The Urban Lawyer* 21, no. 2: 307–349.

Office of Planning Research. State of California. 1992. *The California Planners 1992 Book of Lists*. North Highlands, Calif.: California Department of General Services. March.

Roberts, Thomas E. 1986. "Inclusionary Zoning." In *Zoning and Land Use Controls*, edited by Eric Damian Kelly. New York: Matthew Bender. Chapter 3A.

Saba, Michael. 2000. Senior Planner, Portland, Oregon, Planning Bureau. Telephone interview. 10 January.

Salkin, Patricia. 1993. "Barriers to Affordable Housing: Are Land-Use Controls the Scapegoat?" *Land Use Law & Zoning Digest* 45, no. 4: 3-7.

Schwartz, S. and Johnston, R. 1983. "Inclusionary Housing Programs." *Journal of the American Planning Association* 49, no. 1: 3-21.

Seattle, City of. Department of Construction and Land Use. 1993. *Director's Rule 20-93. Public Benefit Features: Guidelines for Evaluating Bonus and TDR Projects, Administrative Procedures and Submittal Requirements in Downtown Zones*. Seattle, Washington.

_____. 2000. *Toward A Sustainable Seattle*. (Available at: www.ci.seattle.wa.us/planning/CompPlan/HomeCP.htm)

Seyfried, Warren R. 1991. "Measuring the Feasibility of a Zoning Bonus." *Journal of the American Planning Association* 57, no. 3: 348-56.

Slachetka, Stan. 2000. Principal, Burgess Associates. Telephone interview. 4 January.

Smith, Tom. 1999. Assistant Commissioner, Chicago Department of Planning and Development. Telephone interview. 16 September.

Swope, Christopher. 2000. "Little House in the Suburbs." *Governing* (April). (Available at: www.governing.com/4house.htm)

U.S. National Commission on Urban Problems. 1969. *Building the American City: Report to Congress and to the President of the United States*. Washington, D.C.: U.S. Government Printing Office.

Walljasper, Jay. 1999. "A Fair Share in Suburbia." *The Nation*. 25 January. (Available at: www.co.mo.md.us/hca/Housing/MPDU/NationsArt.htm)

Weinstein, Alan. 1994. "Incentive Zoning." In *Zoning and Land Use Controls*, edited by Eric Damian Kelly. New York: Matthew Bender. Chapter 8.

Wheaton, Linda. 1999. Housing Policy Specialist, California Department of Housing and Community Development. Telephone interview. 12 October 12.

White, S. Mark. 1992. *Affordable Housing: Proactive and Reactive Planning Strategies*. Planning Advisory Service Report No. 441. Chicago: American Planning Association. December.

Wittenberg, Jason. 1999. Planner, Minneapolis Planning Department. Facsimile to author. 24 May.

Appendix

1. Premium (Bonus) Provisions in the Minneapolis, Minnesota, Zoning Code

2. A Draft of Model Statute Governing the Use of Incentive Zoning

3. An Excerpt from the American Planning Association Policy Guide on Affordable Housing

PREMIUM (BONUS) PROVISIONS IN THE MINNEAPOLIS, MINNESOTA, ZONING CODE

Title 20 (Zoning Code)

Chapter 549 (Downtown Districts)

Article II (Floor Area Ratio Premiums)

549.220. Floor area ratio premiums.

The following floor area ratio premiums shall be available as specified in Table 549-4, Maximum Floor Area Ratio Premiums in the Downtown Districts [see below], subject to the provisions of this article, provided all other requirements of this zoning ordinance are met:

Urban open space, outdoor, subject to the following standards:

- Outdoor open space shall comprise at least 50 feet of street frontage. Small outdoor open space shall contain not less than 5,000 contiguous square feet. Large outdoor open space shall contain not less than 7,500 contiguous square feet.

- Outdoor open space shall be easily accessible from the adjacent sidewalk and shall contain lighting for nighttime illumination.

- Outdoor open space shall be located near building entrances. Not less than 40 percent of the first-floor facade facing the outdoor open space shall include windows of clear or lightly tinted glass that allow views into and out of the building at eye level.

- Outdoor open space shall be paved with materials that exceed city standards for sidewalk finishes and shall be landscaped with not less than 1 permanent canopy tree and not less than 5 shrubs for each 1,000 square feet of open space. All landscaping shall comply with the plant material and installation standards as specified in Chapter 530, Site Plan Review. Outdoor open space may include additional sidewalk area where the existing sidewalk is less then 15 feet wide. The remainder of the area shall be covered with turf grass, native grasses, or other perennial flowering plants.

- Outdoor open space shall be open to the sky and located to maximize the access of sunlight, except that up to 30 percent of the space may include a covered arcade with a minimum height of 28 feet.

- Outdoor open space shall be designed to encourage use by the general public through the provision of facilities and features including convenient and comfortable seating at a rate of not less than 1 seat per 200 square feet of open space, tables, trash receptacles, plants, water features, and areas for public entertainment or public display of art or cultural exhibits.

- Outdoor open space may contain tables and facilities for food service, but a majority of the space shall be available for general public use without charge.

- The outdoor open space shall be open to the general public at least during the normal business hours of the surrounding area.

- The outdoor open space shall be maintained in good order for the life of the principal structure.

Urban open space, indoor, subject to the following standards:

- Indoor open space shall be located at street level and shall be not more than 3 feet above or below the level of the sidewalk. Small indoor open space shall contain not less than 5,000 contiguous square feet. Large indoor open space shall contain not less than 7,500 contiguous square feet.

- Indoor open space shall be clearly visible and easily accessible from adjacent sidewalks or streets. Walls of an indoor open space area facing sidewalks or an outdoor open space area shall provide a clear view between interior and exterior space.

- Indoor open space shall include an average height not less than 35 feet and a minimum height of 20 feet, and shall include natural light through a glazed roof or windows at a level sufficient to sustain a variety of plants and trees.

- Indoor open space shall be designed to encourage use by the general public through the provision of facilities and features including convenient and comfortable seating at a rate of not less than 1 seat per 200 square feet of open space, tables, trash receptacles, plants and trees, water features, drinking fountains and toilet facilities, and areas for public entertainment or public display of art or cultural exhibits. Not less than 20 percent of the open space shall consist of landscaping or landscaping and water features.

- Indoor open space may contain tables and facilities for food service, but a majority of the space shall be available for general public use without charge. Food preparation areas shall not qualify as required space.

- The indoor open space shall be open to the general public at least during the normal business hours of the surrounding area.

- The indoor open space shall be maintained in good order for the life of the principal structure.

Interior through-block connection, subject to the following standards:

- The connection shall connect two public streets on opposite sides of the block, or shall connect a public street to an urban open space on the opposite side of the block, or shall connect two urban open spaces on opposite sides of the block, or shall connect to another interior through-block connection. In addition, on developments involving less than one-half block, the interior through-block connection may connect 2 public streets on opposite sides of the block in combination with corridors in 1 or more buildings.

- The connection shall be located not more than 3 feet above or below the level of the sidewalk, shall have a minimum interior clear width of 12 feet and a minimum height of 12 feet. The maximum interior through-block connection premium shall be increased by 1 where the interior through-block connection has a minimum interior clear width of 16 feet.

- The connection shall be open to the general public at least during the normal business hours of the surrounding area.

- The connection entrances shall be clearly visible from adjacent sidewalks or streets.

- The connection shall be maintained in good order for the life of the principal structure.

Skyway connection, subject to the following standards:

- The skyway shall connect two blocks on opposite sides of the street.

- The bottom of the skyway shall be a minimum of 16 feet, 6 inches above the street. If street lights are removed, street lighting shall be provided at the bottom of the skyway.

- Skyways and connecting corridors shall have a minimum interior clear width of 12 feet. Skyways shall be no wider than 30 feet. The maximum skyway premium shall be increased by 1 where the skyway and connecting corridor have a minimum interior clear width of 16 feet.

- Skyways shall be single story and designed to be horizontally level with the street. Changes in grade shall be accommodated so that the skyway appears level from the exterior.

- Except where crossing streets and alleys, skyways shall be located within private property.

- At least 80 percent of the vertical enclosure of the skyway shall be windows of clear or lightly tinted glass that allow views into and out of the skyway.

- Skyways shall be designed to facilitate access between street and skyway levels. Elevators, stairs, and escalators linking the street and skyway levels shall be conveniently located with clear directional signs.

- Skyways shall be heated to a minimum of 55 degrees in winter and ventilated to not exceed outdoor temperatures in the summer.

- The skyway shall be open to the general public at least during the hours recommended by the skyway advisory board and approved by the city council.

- The skyway shall be maintained in good order for the life of the principal structure.

Transit facility, subject to the following standards:
- The transit facility shall be located at a transit stop location approved by the planning director in consultation with the city engineer. The maximum transit facility premium shall be increased by 1 where the transit facility is located at an approved light rail transit stop.

- The transit facility shall be open to the general public at least during the normal hours of transit service.

- The transit facility shall be similar to the principal structure in design and materials, shall be weather protected, heated, and lighted, and shall contain at least 2 entries.

- The transit facility shall be clearly visible from the street and sidewalk, and transit users shall be able to see oncoming transit vehicles from the facility.

- The transit facility shall contain a combination of leaning rails and seating for at least 30 percent of projected peak demand, trash receptacles, and connections for transit schedule monitors.

- The transit facility shall be maintained in good order for the life of the principal structure.

Street-level retail uses, subject to the following standards:
- Retail uses shall be limited to Retail Sales and Services uses and Food and Beverages uses included in Table 549-1 Principal Uses in the Downtown Districts.

- Retail uses shall extend along at least 60 percent of the building wall fronting on any street.

- Each retail use shall have at least 1 separate entrance from the sidewalk.

- Street-level uses shall include awnings or canopies to provide protection to pedestrians and to emphasize individual uses and building entrances.

- At least 40 percent of the first floor facade that faces a public street, sidewalk, or parking lot shall be windows or doors of clear or lightly tinted glass that allow views into and out of the building at eye level, except within the NM Nicollet Mall Overlay District, where such district standards shall apply.

- The street-level retail space shall be maintained in good order for the life of the principal structure.

Public art, subject to the following standards:

- The art shall be valued at not less than one-fourth of 1 percent of the capital cost of the principal structure.

- The art shall be located where it is highly visible to the public. If the art is located indoors, such space shall meet the minimum requirements for an indoor open space, interior through-block connection or skyway connecting corridor, as specified in this article.

- The art shall be maintained in good order for the life of the principal structure.

Freight loading terminal, subject to the following standards:

- All freight loading facilities shall be located entirely below grade or entirely enclosed within the principal structure served.

- The freight loading facilities shall be designed to meet the needs and requirements of all uses on the zoning lot.

- The freight loading facility shall be maintained in good order for the life of the principal structure.

Sidewalk widening, subject to the following standards:

- The existing sidewalk shall be less than 15 feet wide.

- The widened sidewalk shall be at least 15 feet wide, open to the sky, paved with materials that meet or exceed city standards for sidewalk finishes, and shall include the provision of street trees as approved by the planning director.

- The widened sidewalk shall be maintained in good order for the life of the principal structure.

Mixed-use residential, subject to the following standards:

- At least 10 percent of the gross floor area of the principal structure shall be occupied by dwelling units.

- The dwelling units shall be located above the first floor.

- The dwelling units shall be maintained in good order for the life of the principal structure.

Historic preservation, subject to the following standards:

- The structure shall be a locally designated historic structure or shall be determined to be eligible to be locally designated as a historic structure, as provided in Chapter 34 of the Minneapolis Code of Ordinances, Heritage Preservation Commission.

- The historic structure, if undesignated, shall be subject to the same restrictions that are applicable to locally designated historic structures and the recommendations contained in The Secretary of the Interior's Standards for Rehabilitation.

- The historic structure shall be rehabilitated pursuant to the applicable guidelines of the heritage preservation commission and the recommendations contained in The Secretary of the Interior's Standards for Rehabilitation, if necessary.

- The historic structure shall be maintained in good order for the life of the principal structure.

TABLE 549–4
MAXIMUM FLOOR AREA RATIO PREMIUMS IN THE DOWNTOWN DISTRICTS[1]

Premium Type	Zoning District and Premium Value			
	B4–2	B4–1 & B4S–2	B4S–1	B4C–1, 2
Urban Open space, small	4.0	3.0	2.0	—
Urban Open space, large	8.0	6.0	4.0	—
Interior through-block connection	1.0 or 2.0	1.0 or 2.0	1.0 or 2.0	1.0 or 2.0
Skyway connection	1.0 or 2.0	1.0 or 2.0	1.0 or 2.0	—
Transit facility	2.0 or 3.0	2.0 or 3.0	2.0 pr 3.0	2.0 or 3.0
Street-level retail	2.0	1.0	1.0	—
Public art	2.0	2.0	1.0	1.0
Freight loading terminal	2.0	2.0	2.0	2.0
Sidewalk widening	2.0	2.0	1.0	1.0
Mixed-use residential	4.0	3.0	—	2.0
Historic preservation	4.0	3.0	2.0	2.0

[1]Less than the maximum premium may be approved where the amenity includes alternatives to the standards of this article, pursuant to Section 549.240.

B4 = Downtown Business District; B4S = Downtown Service District; B4C = Downtown Commercial District

DRAFT OF A MODEL INCENTIVE ZONING STATUTE

Excerpted from the preliminary final draft (July 2000) of Chapter 9 of the Growing Smart[SM] Legislative Guidebook (Chicago: American Planning Association, forthcoming). Section numbers in brackets refer to other sections within the Legislative Guidebook. Other numbers in brackets (e.g., [five] years) are amounts suggested by the authors of the model. An extensive commentary on this part of the Guidebook has been incorporated into the text of this PAS Report and is therefore not repeated here.

The model statute in Section 9-501 below is an adaptation and refinement of the well-drafted California statute that requires local governments to grant density bonuses of at least 25 percent, plus an additional incentive(s) or equivalent financial incentive to developers of affordable housing. In contrast to the California statute, which distinguishes between the types or categories of affordable housing (i.e., between low-income, very-low-income, and senior citizen housing), the model below makes no such differentiation, giving that discretion to local governments. The developer is required to enter into a development agreement with the local government that will formalize the manner in which the affordable housing is to be kept affordable and other administrative details relating to the project. The model statute also authorizes development incentives for increased nonresidential floor area for provision of "public benefit amenities," such as plazas, parks, and open space, access to transit stations, overhead weather protection, and street arcades. A public benefit amenity may also include provision of affordable housing as part of a nonresidential development for which a density bonus may be granted. A local government may also adopt a "uniform incentives ordinance" that addresses both provision of affordable housing and dedication of open space and/or provision of community design amenities.

APA's evaluation of the California statute has determined that, if such program is to be successful at the local level, it is necessary to have a long-term commitment to the program by the local government as well as a dedicated source of funds. Monies such as revenues from tax increment financing (TIF) initiatives and federal community development block grant (CDBG) programs are essential sources to provide subsidies for affordable housing. (See the Petaluma and San Jose case studies in Part 3 of this report.)

9-501 Land-Use Incentives for Affordable Housing, Community Design, and Open Space Dedication; Unified Incentives Ordinance

(1) The legislative body of a local government, in the manner for the adoption and amendment of land development regulations pursuant to Section [8-103 or cite to some other provision, such as a municipal charter or state statute governing the adoption of ordinances]:

(a) shall adopt and amend an ordinance that authorizes incentives for the provision of affordable housing; and

(b) may adopt and amend an ordinance that authorizes incentives for open space dedication and provision of public benefit amenities.

(2) The purpose of this Section is to authorize the adoption and amendment of:

(a) an affordable housing incentives ordinance in order to respond to and accommodate present and future needs for affordable housing;

(b) a community design and open space incentives ordinance to provide additional amenities for public use or benefit in new development that carry out goals and policies of a local government identified in its local comprehensive plan; and

(c) a unified incentives ordinances that incorporates subparagraphs (a) and (b) above.

(3) As used in this Section:

(a) "Affordable Housing" means housing that has a sales price or rental amount that is within the means of a household that may occupy moderate- or low-income housing. In the case of dwelling units for sale, housing that is affordable means housing in which annual housing costs constitute no more than [28] percent of such gross annual household income for a household of the size that may occupy the unit in question. In the case of dwelling units for rent, housing that is affordable means housing for which the affordable rent is no more than [30] percent of such gross annual household income for a household of the size that may occupy the unit in question.

(b) "Affordable Housing Development" means any housing development that is subsidized by the federal, state, or local government, or any housing development in which at least [20] percent of the dwelling units are subject to covenants or restrictions that require such dwelling units to be sold or rented at prices that preserve them as affordable housing pursuant to this Section.

(c) "Affordable Housing Incentives" mean a density bonus and other development incentives granted under an affordable housing incentive ordinance pursuant to this Section.

(d) "Affordable Rent" means monthly housing expenses, including a reasonable allowance for utilities, for affordable housing units that are for rent to low- or moderate-income households.

(e) "Affordable Sales Price" means a sales price at which low- or moderate-income households can qualify for the purchase of affordable housing, calculated on the basis of underwriting standards of mortgage financing available for the housing development.

(f) "Bonusable Area" means space that is occupied by a public benefit amenity and that is determined by the local government to satisfy requirements under its land development regulations for additional gross floor area or dwelling units.

(g) "Bonus Ratio" means the ratio of additional square feet of non-residential floor area granted per square foot of bonusable area.

(h) "Density Bonus" means the percentage of density increase granted over the otherwise maximum allowable net density under the applicable zoning ordinance as of the date of the application to the local government for incentives by a developer. The density bonus applicable to affordable housing shall be at least a 25 percent increase, and shall apply to the site of the affordable housing development.

Commentary: *California communities offer density bonuses well in excess of 25 percent., in some cases as high as 150 to 175 percent. See Robert A. Johnston, Seymour I. Schwartz, Geoffey A. Wandesforde-Smith, and Michael Caplan, "Selling Zoning: Do Density Bonuses for Moderate-Cost Housing Work?"* Land Use Law & Zoning Digest 42, no. 8 *(August 1990): 3-9.*

(i) "Development Agreement" means a development agreement authorized by Section [8-701].

(j) "Development Incentives" mean any of the following:
1. reductions in building setback requirements;

2. reductions or waivers of impact fees, application fees for development permits, utility tap-in fees, or other dedications or exactions;.

3. reductions in minimum lot area, width, or depth;

4. reductions in required parking spaces per dwelling unit;

5. increased maximum lot coverage;

6. increased maximum building height and/or stories;

7. reductions in minimum building separation requirements, provided that such reductions do not conflict with building code requirements of the state or the local government, as applicable;

8. reductions or waivers of public or nonpublic improvements;

9. approval by the legislative body of a local government of mixed-use zoning in conjunction with the housing project if commercial, office, industrial, or other land uses will contribute significantly to the economic feasibility of the housing development and if the mixed-use zoning is consistent with the local comprehensive plan;

10. authorization for the affordable housing development to include nonresidential uses, provided such uses or such authorization is consistent with the local comprehensive plan;

12. authorization for the affordable housing to be located in a nonresidential zoning district, provided such authorization is consistent with the comprehensive plan; or

13. other incentives proposed by the developer of an affordable housing project or by the local government that result in identifiable cost reductions for affordable housing, including direct financial aid by the local government in the form of a loan or grant to subsidize or provide low-interest financing for on- or off-site improvements, land, or construction costs.

(k) "Floor Area Ratio" means the ratio of the maximum gross floor area on a lot or parcel to the area of the lot or parcel that is permitted pursuant to the land development regulations of a local government.

(l) "Housing Cost" means the sum of actual or projected monthly payments for any of the following associated with for-sale affordable housing units: principal and interest on a mortgage loan, including any loan insurance fees; property taxes and assessments; fire and casualty insurance; property maintenance and repairs; homeowner association fees; and a reasonable allowance for utilities.

(m) "Housing Development" means construction, including rehabilitation, projects consisting of five or more residential units, including single-family, two-family, and multiple-family residences for sale or rent.

(n) "Incentives" mean one or more of the following:
1. affordable housing incentives;
2. bonus ratio; and
3. density bonus.

(o) "Low-Income Housing" means housing that is affordable, according to the federal Department of Housing and Urban Development, for either home ownership or rental, and that is occupied, reserved, or marketed for occupancy by households with a gross household income that does not exceed 50 percent of the median gross household income for households of the same size within the housing region in which the housing is located.

(p) "Moderate-Income Housing" means housing that is affordable, according to the federal Department of Housing and Urban Development, for either home ownership or rental, and that is occupied, reserved, or marketed for occupancy by households with a gross household income that is greater than 50 percent but does not exceed 80 percent of the median gross household income for households of the same size within the housing region in which the housing is located.

(q) "Public Benefit Amenity" means one or more features for public use or benefit contained in a development that will entitle the development to a bonus ratio or a density bonus, as applicable, including, but not limited to:
1. shopping atriums;
2. plazas, parks, and other open spaces;
3. overhead weather protection and street arcades;
4. performing arts theaters;
5. museums;
6. access to transit stations and transit easements;
7. provision of child day-care centers;
8. provision of affordable housing as part of a nonresidential development; and
9. [other].

(r) "Unified Incentives Ordinance" means an ordinance that provides incentives for both:
1. provision of affordable housing; and
2. dedication of open space and/or provision of community design amenities; and that complies with all requirements of this Section for both an affordable housing incentives ordinance and a community design and open space incentives ordinance.

(4) The legislative body of a local government may adopt and amend an affordable housing incentives ordinance only after it has adopted a local comprehensive plan that contains:

(a) a housing element pursuant to Section [7-207]; and

(b) a policy in written and/or mapped form that encourages affordable housing incentives.

(5) The legislative body of a local government may adopt and amend a community design and open space incentives ordinance only after it has adopted a local comprehensive plan that contains:

(a) a housing element pursuant to Section [7-207] if a density bonus for residential development for the public benefit amenity of a plaza, park, or other open spaces is authorized; and

(b) a community design element pursuant to Section [7-214] if any other type of bonus ratio is authorized; and

(c) a policy in written and/or mapped form that describes the relationship between the applicable public benefit amenities and the density bonus or bonus ratio and supports the granting of such density bonus or bonus ratio.

(6) An affordable housing incentive ordinance, a community design and open space incentives ordinance, or a unified incentives ordinance shall include the following minimum provisions:

(a) a citation to enabling authority to adopt and amend the ordinance;

(b) a statement of purpose consistent with the purposes of land development regulations pursuant to Section [8-102(2)] and with the purposes of this Section;

(c) a statement of consistency with the local comprehensive plan that is based on findings made pursuant to Section [8-104];

(d) definitions, as appropriate for such words or terms contained in the affordable housing incentive ordinance. Where this Chapter or Section defines words or terms, the ordinance shall incorporate those definitions, either directly or by reference;

(e) procedures for the review of applications for incentives;

(f) a requirement that every developer that is to receive incentives shall enter into a development agreement with the local government;

(g) designation of an officer or body to review and approve applications for incentives; and

(h) provisions for enforcement, including the issuance of certificates of compliance.

(7) An affordable housing incentives ordinance or a unified incentives ordinance shall also include the following minimum provisions:

(a) a requirement that, where a developer proposes a housing development within the jurisdiction of the local government, the local government shall provide the developer with affordable housing incentives for the production of affordable housing within the development if the developer meets the requirements set forth in paragraphs (11) and (12) below; and

(b) provisions to ensure that once affordable housing is built through subsidies or other means as part of a housing development, its availability will be maintained through measures that establish income qualifications for affordable housing renters or purchasers, promote affirmative marketing measures, and regulate the price and rent, including resale price, of affordable housing units.

(8) A community design and open space incentives ordinance or a unified incentives ordinance shall also include the following minimum provisions:

(a) a statement of the types or categories or public benefit amenities for which a bonus ratio or density bonus shall be authorized, the amount of the respective bonus ratio or density bonus, and the zoning use district or overlay district to which public benefit amenity and the respective bonus ratio or density bonus apply;

(b) locational and other development standards for the public benefit amenities, including a statement of the minimum bonusable area that a public benefit amenity must contain in order to be eligible for a bonus ratio or a density bonus; and

(c) requirements for permanent public access to the public benefit amenity, including signage indicating the nature of the public access, secured by either:

1. a conveyance of the plaza, park, or other open space, or access to transit stations or transit easements, to the local government or appropriate governmental unit as a public use as a condition of approval of the development permit, provided that the conveyance is in a form approved by the attorney of the local government or governmental unit; or

2. where the public benefit amenity will not be owned by the local government or another governmental unit, provisions in the development agreement requiring permanent maintenance by the property owner, except that permanent public access may be limited to normal business hours.

(9) An affordable housing incentives ordinance or a unified incentives ordinance may require that any new housing development within the jurisdiction of the local government contain at least [15] percent affordable housing if such a requirement is consistent with a policy contained in the local comprehensive plan. The incentives offered to the developer, whether density bonuses, development incentives, or both, shall be at least of equivalent financial value to the cost of making the affordable housing units affordable.

(10) A community design and open space incentives ordinance or a unified incentives ordinance may:

(a) include a manual of graphic and written design guidelines to assist developers in the preparation of applications for community design and open space incentives, but such guidelines shall be advisory only;

(b) include a statement of the maximum bonusable area that a public benefit amenity may contain in order to be eligible for a bonus ratio or a density bonus;

(c) include a provision that allows the developer to provide the public benefit amenity offsite as a condition of receiving a bonus ratio or density bonus, including standards of proximity of the development to the off-site public benefit amenity; and

(d) be adopted as an overlay district to all or portions of existing zoning use districts. The boundaries of the overlay district shall be shown on the zoning map pursuant to Section [8-201(3)(o)].

(11) Where a developer proposes a housing development that is to be an affordable housing development, the local government shall either:

(a) grant a density bonus and at least one development incentive, unless the local government makes a written finding that the development incentive is not necessary to reduce the price or rent of the dwelling units in order to ensure that they are affordable housing; or

(b) provide, in lieu of subparagraph (a) above, development incentives of equivalent financial value based upon the land cost per dwelling unit. The value of such equivalent development incentives shall equal at least the land cost per dwelling units that would result from a density bonus and shall contribute significantly to the economic feasibility of providing the affordable housing units.

(12) The development agreement entered into between the developer of a housing development that is to be an affordable housing development and the local government shall include provisions to ensure the availability of affordable housing for sale or rent.

(a) The development agreement shall provide for a period of availability for affordable housing as follows:

1. Newly constructed low- and moderate-income sales and rental dwelling units shall be subject to affordability controls for a period of not less than [15] years, which period may be renewed pursuant to the development agreement;

2. Rehabilitated owner-occupied single-family dwelling units that are improved to code standard shall be subject to affordability controls for at least [5] years.

3. Rehabilitated renter-occupied dwelling units that are improved to code standard shall be subject to affordability controls on re-rental for at least [10] years.

4. Any dwelling unit created through the conversion of a non-residential structure shall be considered a new dwelling unit and shall be subject to affordability controls as delineated in subparagraph (a) 1 above.

5. Affordability controls on owner- or renter-occupied accessory apartments shall be applicable for a period of at least [5] years.

6. Alternative living arrangements not otherwise described in this subparagraph shall be controlled in a manner deemed suitable to the local government and shall provide assurances that such arrangements will house low- and moderate-income households for at least [10] years.

(b) In the case of for-sale housing developments, the development agreement shall include the following affordability controls governing the initial sale and use and any resale:

1. All conveyances of newly constructed affordable housing dwelling units subject to the affordable housing incentives ordinance that are for sale shall contain a deed restriction and mortgage lien, which shall be recorded with the county [recorder of deeds]. Any restrictions on future resale shall be included in the deed restriction as a condition of approval enforceable through legal and equitable remedies.

2. Affordable housing units shall, upon initial sale, and resale in the period covered by the development agreement, be sold to eligible low- or moderate-income households at an affordable sales price and housing cost.

3. Affordable housing units shall be occupied by eligible low- or moderate- income households during the period covered by the development agreement.

(c) In the case of rental housing developments, the development agreement shall include the following affordability controls governing the use of affordable housing units during the use restriction period:

1. rules and procedures for qualifying tenants, establishing affordable rent, filling vacancies, and maintaining affordable housing rental units for qualified tenants;

2. requirements that owners verify tenant incomes and maintain books and records to demonstrate compliance with the agreement and with the ordinance;

3. requirements that owners submit an annual report to the local government demonstrating compliance with the agreement and with the ordinance.

(d) The development agreement shall include a schedule that provides for the affordable housing units to be built concurrently with the units that are not subject to affordability controls.

(13) The approval of incentives shall constitute a development permit. The incentives shall be part of the unified development permit review process established pursuant to Section [10-201].

(14) This Section does not limit or require the provision of direct financial aid by the local government, the provision of publicly owned land, or the waiver or reduction of fees, including impact fees pursuant to Section [8-602], or of dedication or exaction requirements pursuant to Section [8-601].

(15) The [state planning agency or state department of development] shall by [date] prepare and distribute a model affordable housing incentives ordinance and related guidelines to assist local governments in complying with this Section.

EXCERPTS FROM THE AMERICAN PLANNING ASSOCIATION POLICY GUIDE ON HOUSING

This is an edited excerpt from the American Planning Association's Policy Guide on Housing that pertains to issues presented in this report; namely, housing supply and demand, housing location, and the use of comprehensive planning, zoning, and subdivision controls as a means for improving housing supply and affordability in a region or local jurisdiction. The full policy guide on housing is available on the APA web site at www.planning.org.

Adopted by the Chapter Delegate Assembly, April 25, 1999
Ratified by the Board of Directors, April 26, 1999
This Policy Guide is dedicated to the late Marsha Ritzdorf, planner, educator, and tireless advocate for social equity.

FINDINGS

1. There were 97.7 million households in the U.S. in 1995. Of these, 63.5 million were owner-occupants and 34.2 million were renters. Almost one-third (31 percent) of all households lived in central cities, while another 31 percent lived in suburbs. Thirty-eight percent lived in rural areas.[1]

Housing Quality and Housing Costs

2. Homeowners as well as renters face problems with housing quality and affordability. According to the American Housing Survey, 16.1 million renters and 15.9 million homeowners experienced moderate or severe housing problems in 1995. Moderate housing problems include housing costs greater than 30 percent of household income, overcrowding, and moderately inadequate housing conditions.[2]

Severe housing problems, on the other hand, include housing costs greater than 50 percent of household income and/or severely inadequate housing conditions. Households spending more than 30 percent of income for housing have little money available to meet other basic needs, such as food and clothing, much less disposable income to contribute to the economy.

3. Affordable rental units are diminishing in number. Between 1993 and 1995, 900,000 rental units affordable to households with incomes at or below 50 percent of area median were lost due to expiration of public subsidies, demolition of sub-standard subsidized units, and redevelopment.[3,4] From 1995 to 1997, the federal government issued no new Section 8 Certificates or Vouchers to increase the num-ber of renter households assisted through this program or to offset expiring pro-ject-based subsidies. The 1998 and 1999 HUD budget provided the first increases in new Section 8 Vouchers, intended for welfare to work transitions. Nevertheless, these allocations do not begin to offset the impact of expiring subsidies for pri-vately owned low-rent housing.[5]

4. Research demonstrates that affordable housing does not negatively affect sur-rounding single-family property values. In some instances, affordable housing de-velopment can actually trigger increases in surrounding property values.[6]

. . .

Jobs/Housing Balance
9. Low-income households remain concentrated in central cities while new low-wage jobs are created in suburbs. One of every five urban families lived in poverty in 1996 compared to fewer than one in 10 families in the suburbs. From 1991 to 1994, 87 percent of new low-skilled jobs were created outside of central cities.[7]

. . .

GENERAL POLICIES
General Policy 1. Planners should strive to identify and address housing needs in urban, suburban, and rural areas.

General Policy 2. Planners should promote, through comprehensive plans, zoning codes, and subdivision regulations, housing stock in a wide range of prices, with a variety of types and configurations, to offer choice in location, type, and afford-ability to all members of the community.

. . .

General Policy 4. Planners should help to eliminate housing discrimination in their communities.

General Policy 5. Planners should work to minimize the economic stratification of cities by income level, segregating the poor into one district, the middle-class into another, and the rich into yet another. Although this has been federal policy for more than 20 years, its implementation at the local level has been slow.

. . .

General Policy 7. Planners should promote better balance between the location of jobs and housing.

. . .

General Policy 9. Planners must work with nonprofit as well as for-profit residen-tial developers to implement housing goals.

SPECIFIC POLICIES
1. Planning
a. Residential development is a principal feature of communities, and should be represented in the comprehensive plan not only as a land use but also as an im-portant element of community vitality and economic health. Planners should en-courage their jurisdictions to develop and maintain a comprehensive plan housing element that analyzes housing needs for all types and price ranges, and recom-mends specific measures to address gaps in the housing supply.

b. Planners should help preserve the environment by encouraging residential construction that is consistent with the principles of smart growth. Planners should promote housing that is energy efficient and does not place undue de-mands on the environment. Regional plans should promote compact and clus-tered development patterns while discouraging leapfrogging and sprawl development.

c. Planners should encourage their jurisdictions to adopt and implement plans and policies that reflect federal and state requirements regarding housing, that promote housing choice and affordability across all price ranges, and that make effective use of federal, state, and local programs and incentives to meet housing needs not adequately addressed through the marketplace.

d. APA National and Chapters should support national, state, and local policies that contribute to residential stability, affordability, and choice. These policies should not be limited to traditional homeownership models, but embrace nontraditional forms of homeownership, such as limited equity cooperatives, mutual housing, and community land trusts. Similarly, provision should be made for quality rental housing, not only through traditional multifamily forms, but also through single-family, mixed-use, and mixed-tenure development.

e. Planners should encourage housing strategies to revitalize older urban neighborhoods, while taking steps to minimize displacement of existing businesses and residents. Such strategies might include mixed-use and infill development, mixed-income housing, homeownership zones, urban homesteading, and housing rehabilitation.

f. Planners should promote infill housing strategies that encourage compatibility with existing housing stock. Planners should be at the forefront of ensuring that housing not only has good immediate utility, but also represents a long-term, value-added investment to the neighborhood and the larger community.

g. Planners should use their technical skills to weigh objectively whether rehabilitation or clearance and redevelopment of severely blighted neighborhoods presents the most viable solution to urban blight. In making such an evaluation, planners should involve neighborhood residents and institutions in the planning process, and examine whether financing is in place to complete redevelopment activities after initial clearance of the site.

h. Planners should engage neighborhoods in planning for revitalization, making use of collaborative planning tools and techniques that bring a wide range of interests and voices to the table, and that empower citizens to exercise influence in and access to the policy development process. (See APA Policy Guide on Neighborhood Collaborative Planning, adopted April 1998.)

i. APA National and chapters should encourage and facilitate collaboration and coordination among planning, housing, and code enforcement trade associations and interest groups.

j. APA National and Chapters recognize that housing is a regional issue in metropolitan areas, usually requiring interjurisdictional dialogue and cooperation. APA National and Chapters should support a regional fair-share distribution of affordable housing, particularly in proximity to moderate- and low-wage jobs.

. . .

3. Affordable Housing
a. APA National and Chapters should collaborate with nonprofit and for-profit housing providers to educate citizens and elected officials about affordable housing and work to eliminate negative perceptions and stereotypes. Zoning requests for residential development affordable to low-income households should not be arbitrarily denied.

b. APA National and Chapters should encourage national, state, and local initiatives designed to preserve and expand affordable housing opportunities at a variety of income levels. Planners should work to ensure that scarce housing subsidies are used to provide long-term benefits to those in need of assistance. In general, capital subsidies for construction or acquisition of housing should also be accompanied by measures that ensure long-term affordability. (See APA Policy Guide on The Supply of Public and Subsidized Housing, adopted October 18, 1991.)

c. Planners should expand affordable housing opportunities by facilitating the development and preservation of accessory apartments, cluster housing, elder cottages, manufactured housing, mixed-income housing, shared residences, and single room occupancy (SRO) developments.

d. APA National and Chapters should work to preserve the federal Low-Income Housing Tax Credit, a critical tool for affordable housing finance, and to encourage accountability in the management of LIHTC projects.

e. APA National and Chapters should work to renew and expand the availability of federal funding for Section 8 Certificates and Vouchers or alternative models of direct rent subsidy to enable low-income households to afford decent housing in the private market. Alternative models should not be limited to federally supported initiatives but also embrace state and local programs.

f. APA National and Chapters should support, based on local conditions, controls on conversion of rental housing to condominiums where it affects the availability of affordable housing; controls on unreasonable increases in rent; and requirements for just cause for eviction of renters. These tools should remain available to local governments for use in response to locally defined needs, and not preempted by state or federal legislation.

g. APA National and Chapters should work with state, federal, and local governments to facilitate economic development strategies that will yield living wage jobs and enable families and individuals to afford housing without the necessity of additional public subsidies and incentives.

h. APA National and Chapters should support and promote programs and incentives that encourage private and nonprofit development of affordable housing to supplement publicly owned and managed housing, and that complement local housing delivery systems. These measures include density bonuses, land donations, low-income housing tax credits, and commercial linkage impact fees.

i. APA National and Chapters should support, based upon local conditions, the provision of affordable housing for farm employees and their families, and other seasonal workers.

. . .

6. Jobs/housing Balance
a. APA National and Chapters should work to preserve existing housing stock near major employers in order to reduce transportation and air quality problems, and create housing opportunities in close proximity to new suburban, exurban, and rural employment centers. Economic development and housing planners, in conjunction with large employers (if feasible), should perform housing impact studies to analyze the availability of affordable housing for their workers in proximity to work locations.

b. APA National and Chapters should emphasize the role of an adequate supply of affordable housing in economic development strategies.

c. APA National and Chapters should encourage employers to invest in their workers and their neighborhoods by supporting employer-assisted housing programs, especially ones that encourage employees to own or rent in the neighborhood adjacent to the employer.

d. APA National and Chapters should support transportation and transit improvements that allow low-income households in central cities to access jobs in surrounding suburbs.

e. APA National and Chapters encourage new employment centers in or near existing residential neighborhoods, provided such development can be accomplished without displacement of existing residents.

f. Local governments should, in coordination with regional planning efforts, identify strategies to meet housing demand generated by economic development.

ENDNOTES

1. National Low Income Housing Coalition, *Advocates Resource Book: Low Income Housing Profile*, 1998.

2. U.S. Department of Housing and Urban Development. "Rental Housing Assistance: The Crisis Continues," April 1998.

3. U.S. Department of Housing and Urban Development. "Rental Housing Assistance: The Crisis Continues, Executive Summary," April 1998.

4. U.S. Department of Housing and Urban Development, *Waiting in Vain; Update on America's Rental Housing Crisis* (Washington, D.C., 1999).

5. Ibid.

6. Ron Smith, ed., *The Las Vegas Metropolitan Area Project* (Las Vegas: The University of Nevada, Las Vegas, 1998), pp.145-66. See also Michael S. Marous, "Low-Income Housing in our Backyards: What Happens to Residential Property Values," *Appraisal Journal* 64: 27-33 and Marco A. Martinez, "Effects of Subsidized and Affordable Housing on Property Values: A Survey of Research" (Sacramento: California Department of Housing and Community Development, 1988); Xavier de Souza Briggs, Joe T. Darden, and Angela Aidala, "In the Wake of Desegregation: Early Impacts of Scattered-Site Public Housing on Neighborhoods in Yonkers, New York," *Journal of the American Planning Association* (Winter 1999): 27-49.

7. U.S. Department of Housing and Urban Development, "The State of the Cities: 1998."